BEYOND BYZANTIUM

BEYOND BYZANTIUM
THE LAST PHASE
OF YEATS'S CAREER

ARRA M. GARAB

 NORTHERN ILLINOIS UNIVERSITY PRESS ■ DeKalb

PR
5907
G3

For Suzanne
and
Varsie, Lisa, and Gary

✳ PREFACE

 This study has grown from my long-standing conviction that the poetry of the last decade of Yeats's career deserves special scrutiny because of its unusual importance in the total scheme of his art. Sensing acutely that these poems written beyond Byzantium were to be his last expressions of self, the aged and dying poet charged them with overwhelming honesty and painful candor, with such tensions and so awesome a sense of finality that we fail to scrutinize them only at the peril of remaining uncertain about the ultimate contours of his life's work.

 Both the distinctive unity of this crucial group of poems and its relevance to the rest of Yeats's work, then, have been among my major concerns. Demonstrating their otherness, I have also tried to stress their complementary function. Following Yeats beyond Byzantium, beyond that sacred city of art that so exquisitely mirrors more than a century of romantic yearning, I have tracked him to realms not of sages and gold but of unfinished men and the dross of their mortal pain.

 Yeats was the chief inheritor of the romantic tradition strong throughout the nineteenth century. He brought the concerns of his romantic heritage deep into our own era; but in so doing he eventually forsook his earlier quest for essence for an equally powerful passion for existence. Herein lies the tragic basis of the final phase of both his art and life. Ever an "enquiring man," in old age Yeats discovered that the only meaningful posture possible for him was that of commitment to the here of his history and the now of his time. Yet always a disquieted romantic and a basically unaccommodated man, he tempered his newly gained existential stance with lust for healthier wholes and rage at their rareness.

I owe the greatest debt in the making of this book to my mentor at Columbia University, William York Tindall. Sustaining me in classes and seminars many years ago, he still continues to do so today even as my own graduate students set forth on their own. Yet, though I savor his sins, I insist that mine are not his.

For help and criticism I am especially indebted to the Reverend Davis Barker, Timothy Hunt, Johnstone Parr, Wilma Reuland, and John Unterecker. I am grateful for generous financial assistance to the research councils of Kent State University and Northern Illinois University. Generosity and good cheer have always marked the work of my research assistant, Glynn Steele; helping me see this book through the press, she found time to help launch me on another.

Completed on 24 April, the anniversary of the martyrdom of a million and a half Armenians by the Turks in 1915, this book is offered to their blessed memory. It is dedicated specifically to my wife and children, who, in the New World far from the historical Byzantium of my forefathers, remain loyal to their ancient and abiding faith.

✳ CONTENTS

INTRODUCTION ✳ A TIME OF TURBULENCE

 THE OLD AGE of a poet is not often a felicitous subject of inquiry: witness Wordsworth "withering into eighty years, honoured and empty-witted."[1] Rarely, indeed, does a poet reveal, as did Yeats, such persistent power of control, such rich capacity for growth. For all his wanderings upon "Hodos Chameliontos," Yeats always attempted to see life steadily and, during the last decade or so of his life, came to see it whole, thereby facing his fundamental identity as a man. This coming to terms with his own humanity, this wholeness of vision which, after great anguish, Yeats finally attained, is the prime concern of this study.

Yeats's long and productive career may be seen as a perpetual metamorphosis. Forever renewing himself, he traveled the winding path of his Hermetic chameleon, pausing periodically to astound his readers with the consummate completeness of his successive transformations. Out of a protracted quarrel with himself—"Myself must I remake"—he fashioned great poetry, which, despite the complexity of its themes and forms, unmistakably displays organic unity. The Yeatsian canon, that impressive "Sacred Book" fifty years in the making, is not under scrutiny here: only its final (and perhaps most exciting) components—the rounding out, as it were, of the whole.

Gravely ill for the better part of the last decade of his life, Yeats in old age turned his perspectives to fundamental concerns. "Indomitable," he cast his mind on the "measurement" and "might" of other days; remembering that he must die, he focused as well on what theology calls "final things"—death, judgment, heaven, and hell. At the same time, he found it necessary to bring within the compass of his art frankly base concerns, matters which he held to be as basic as the eschatological ones. To transcend "immensities," he discovered, it was necessary at times to descend among them—that is, to promote those furious passions and involvements that engage when all else seems tried or untrue. Thus, though his life (as Auden tells us) made him "silly like us," his "gift" (as his last poems show) "survived it all."

"Physical decay" and "mad Ireland" brought out the best and the worst in him. Repeatedly ill with high fever and shortness of breath, he pathetically turned to monkey glands for rejuvenation; eager to "justify those renowned generations," for a time he looked to blue-shirted General O'Duffy for political justification. He survived the "innocent and the beautiful"—what he considered the best of his generation. Lissadell betrayed and Coole about to be sold for taxes,[2] in 1926 he saw Maud Gonne, his Countess Cathleen, lead pickets at the Abbey in a demonstration against The Plough and the Stars. Though he lived to see Lady Gregory and Olivia Shakespear pass away, he managed to replenish his "parish of rich women" by communing and creating with Dorothy Wellesley, a talented gentlewoman whose pretension puffed his own, but whose adulation served as catalyst for his remarkable talent.

Yet for all that, the poetry of these last ten years is a most distinctive achievement. Refreshing because of the vital ground from which they spring, the lyrics of Words for Music Perhaps, Supernatural Songs, and the posthumously published Last Poems strike not only new but often strange and exhilarating notes. We find here poetry of involvement, art sharpened by the press of crowded years and quickened by an artist's tragic sense of mortality. Drawing rein, Yeats "cast a cold eye" not only on death, but on the "manifold illusion" that temporarily sustains when the "heart" cries out "against necessity." Standing his ground, he passed old and new themes before "an old man's eagle eye." To the last, his vision remained honest. Though grounded in antinomies, it forever worked toward resolution; but synthesis, Yeats learned early, grew from dialectical tensions and not from easy answers.

The basic questions, never "answered" but always asked, now seemed more urgent than ever. Yeats's treatment of them, as we would expect, reflects this urgency. We see in his poetry of 1929–1939 such familiar Yeatsian motifs as the relation of body and soul, of life to art, of the artist to his past; the question of artifice versus actuality; the meaning of history, and the ends to which men and all creation move; the memory of "beautiful lofty things" both personal and public, poetic and political. Newer images emerge and soon come to crowd the apocalyptic landscape formed by his heightened imagination. Urgent now are portentous questions concerning the tragic circumstances of existence and the tragic nature of man's fate. "Tragic joy," at once the matrix and the pinnacle of his final, transforming vision, and perhaps Yeats's most significant legacy to our "tired" and "hysterical" age, not only informs two of his best poems, but illuminates as well a cluster of haunting and diverse lyrics.

Yeats's final poems do not merely offer impressive inscapes of experience and imagination. Much of their impressiveness is derived from structures equal to the tasks demanded by his penetrating insights. Once again the forms grow tight, the diction hard and dry. Freer than ever before, the images range far and wide. At times, the accents and tonalities reveal experimentation; sometimes they are drawn from traditions hitherto tapped only imperfectly; always, however, they sound sure. We cannot be complacent before them. Often the natural scene grows dark and desolate, only to be fired suddenly by blazing flashes of wit and light. The mundane and the bizarre, coexisting in perilous equilibrium, form patterns to ponder, to "mark and digest." If the speakers of these poems stare and scorn from lonely aeries of the mind, they engage and convince because their metaphysic towers from stone and clay. As Yeats once said of Donne's poetry, so too must we say of Yeats's final achievement: "His pedantry and his obscenity—the rock and loam of his Eden—but make me more certain that one who is but a man like us all has seen God."[3]

Acutely aware always of the mutability of all things, Yeats devoted great care to the inescapable fact of old age and the general destructiveness of time. From his adolescence on, his work reveals an almost compulsive desire to escape the turbulence of time. Though Yeats reached Byzantium in 1927, scrutiny of his poems shows that he had set sail some forty years earlier. From *The Wanderings of Oisin* to "Sailing to Byzantium," a significant number of Yeats's poetic speakers, unable or unwilling to come to terms with the life within and around them, flee or are summoned to flee the bitter and debilitating actualities of their psychic and physical environments. Anxious to "shed time's filthy load," they yearn for stasis and release, and thus seek the solace to be found in never-never lands ranging from the storied woods of Arcady and Tir-nan-oge to the golden boughs of Byzantium.

This theme of escape from the conditions and circumstances of mortality is central to an understanding of Yeats's early work, and it lies at the crux of the especially agonizing vacillations of his maturity. Hence, a survey in chapter one of some typical manifestations. Interesting in itself and for the poems it produces, this dominant early motif concerns us here primarily because of the counterstatements to which it eventually leads. Much of the poetry of the last phase of Yeats's career, we shall see, is built on these counterstatements. With "A Dialogue of Self and Soul" (1927–1928) it becomes clear that henceforth the claims of "life" will dominate, that "dying," Yeats too will take "the living world for text." From now on, as Yeats himself explained, the time-befouled "swordsman" will "repudiate" the time-free "saint," "but not"—he was careful to add—"without vacillation."[4]

Chapter two, "The Living World," scans the new scene where the final drama of Yeats's "Sacred Book" is played out. Crazy Jane, Old Tom, and Ribh, precursors of the *personae* of *Last Poems*, are the principal players here. As though taking their cue from the Self's inspiring peroration, they celebrate the "impure ditches" of a world where "Nothing can be sole or whole/That has not been rent." Their world of the "dying generations," for all its corruption and impermanence, is the place where Yeats, after much sailing, finally dropped anchor. Finding his final metaphysical bearings here, here at the age of seventy-one his imagination took fire again.

The remaining chapters are devoted to *Last Poems*. With Yeats's theory of history in the background, chapter three focuses primarily on "The Gyres," and on "tragic joy," Yeats's ultimate posture before the great mutations of time. "Lapis Lazuli," a companion poem, forms the center of the next chapter, a study of the tragic gaiety which allowed Yeats to lift his much-awaited "heroic cry in the midst of despair." [5] Springing from the "abyss" of violent "dread," the "profound philosophy" [6] of this crucial poem enables dread-filled man to rise to the ecstasy of the tragic moment. Governing all of Yeats's final work, it provides the lofty and shaping vision—the ultimate perspective—whereby the absurd and shapeless are made to reveal their meaning.

Chapter five embraces many poems of different sorts. What they have in common is that they all display Yeats seeking new and stimulating insights by assuming postures that he considered appropriate to the aged and, more importantly, relevant to his own circumstances. As we would expect, many of these poems are about old age itself; all, however, reveal masks characteristic of Yeats's amazingly active and "many-minded" old age: Lear, Lecher, Fiddler, Faithful Servant, Swift, and the Fool—to isolate the most important. Chapter six, proceeding from an examination in the previous chapter of the influence on Yeats of Gaelic ballads and the sense of Ireland's past—"I am still their servant though all are underground"—shows Yeats the patriot in an almost private pantheon of memories and of the lordly men and women who made them. "The Municipal Gallery Revisited," a remarkable tour de force, is the main text here.

The seventh chapter is on "The Three Bushes" and its six attendant lyrics. These rich lyrics, among the "earthiest" of Yeats's last poems as well as among the most "philosophical," at once display the ways and whys of love while also exploring with great economy and artistry such weightier themes as appearance and reality, the many and the one, man and God. A brief concluding section summarizes my views concerning Yeats's ultimate reconciliation with time.

CHAPTER ONE ✳ CONTEMPLATIONS OF TIME

S HORTLY after his sixty-seventh birthday, having just finished correcting the proofs of the first volume of a projected collected edition of his works, Yeats was "greatly astonished" to discover a remarkable singularity of theme pervading his lyric poetry of nearly half a century. He wrote to his friend Olivia Shakespear: "I keep saying what man is this who . . . says the same thing in so many different ways. My first denunciation of old age I made in *The Wanderings of Usheen* (end of part I) before I was twenty and the same denunciation comes in the last pages of the book."[1] "Denunciation of old age" is indeed a recurring and major motif, and its persistence is one of the most striking features of his poetry. (The word *old* occurs 575 times in Yeats's poems, placing second in the frequency list.[2]) Especially significant is the more basic concern prompting its expression: the ravages wrought by fickle and unfeeling time.

The vexatious problem of time, a traditional theme of Western literature, especially among romantics, plays a crucial role in Yeats's development. More so than most of his contemporaries, Yeats was imbued with what Miguel de Unamuno has termed "the tragic sense of life": Man's most passionate craving is for immortality, yet his most consuming awareness is the reality of death; desperately seeking the abiding, man predicates all his activity on a dream of permanence, yet daily is confronted by his own corruptibility and the transience of all things.

Much of Yeats's work, then, is permeated with responses to the challenge of flux and change. Throughout his career, we find his poetic speakers constantly confronted by the burden of mutability. Fired by a rage for essence, many of them struggle to discover what abides while all else passes away. Pursuit of the noumenally real, that which transcends all phenomenal creation, not only helps to charge Yeats's poetry with much of its energy and tension, but provides the motivating force for their composition as well; for as with others of his lost generation, Yeats believed that in a world beset by uncertainty and branded by the inevitability of change, works of art alone were "certain good." Inheriting a fragmented world left sterile by yet another fall of man in the mid-nineteenth century, he looked to art for succor and salvation. The beatific vision, once the end of human endeavor and a sign of salvation, he sought to revive by the thaumaturgical process of secular artistic activity.

During his earliest creative years his concern with the problem of time lacks focus and perspective, and is devoid of direction except as it provides material for dream and provokes yearnings for escape. In very early poems such as "The Song of the Happy Shepherd" (original version published 1885) and *The Wanderings of Oisin* (first published 1889), his thoughts of time are fixed in "endless reverie" and inward dreaming. In other poems of this period, the ill-fated "Time and the Witch Vivien," for example, they seem to exist in a cultural vacuum, in contexts remote from the immediacies of credible experience.[3]

In "Time and the Witch Vivien" (1889), the denunciation is shrill, melodramatic, and utterly unconvincing. The poem is submerged by prosaic assertiveness, stilted dialogue, bizarre decor, and decadent claptrap. But lightweight though the effort, the young Yeats's theme is unmistakable. Time is all-powerful, and its workings defy human control. Even such an extraordinary person as Vivien, a "witch" gifted with enviable powers, is powerless in her fatal encounter with time.

Vivien, in a "marble-flagged, pillared room," her "magical instruments in one corner," admiringly peers at her image in a fountain until her reverie is interrupted by the entrance of Time, an awkward figure dressed as "an old pedlar" carrying a scythe, hourglass, and black bag, at whom she scoffs and whom she terms "the wrinkled squanderer of human wealth." Patronizingly inquiring about the contents of the bag, she learns that it contains "crutches and grey hairs," whereupon she vehemently refuses to make a purchase. She notes the hourglass, however, and asks to buy it, but when Time refuses to sell, she arranges to roll dice for the coveted object. She loses the game, exclaiming "They're loaded dice. Time always plays/With loaded dice," and then calls for a game of chess in which her stake is "triumph in my many plots" and her forfeit death. "Chance, and not skill, has favoured you, old father!" she cries out the first time she is checked; but checked again and again, she is finally checkmated, whereupon she dies, exclaiming "Already?/Chance hath a skill!"

A related image to that of Vivien gazing at herself in a reflecting pool is found in "The Old Men Admiring Themselves in the Water," a brief poem written shortly after the turn of the century. The theme here, however, is different in that the decrepit old men, already having suffered time's effects, now seem to be filled with a mysterious knowledge. "Everything alters," they say, "All that's beautiful drifts away/Like the waters." The simplicity of this lyric is deceptive. Yeats's attitude is complex, and this complexity is mirrored in the basic ambiguity around which the poem is conceived. Not only is an analogy suggested between the twisted old men and the gnarled thorn-trees, but their mutation is attributed to the action of "the waters," an image both of moving time and of life processes.[4] Their clawlike hands, like their twisted knees, would seem to define physical decrepitude, but the bird image also suggests longevity and the wisdom that comes with time.

The richness of the poem itself is augmented by the ambiguity of the title, where the key word is "admiring." Is the action of the old men foolish? Are they, in their senility, foolishly demonstrating their vanity? Or, in the archaic sense of *admire*, are they regarding the human condition with wonder and astonishment? And "wonder" and "astonishment"—these too are ambiguous states in that they lie beyond mere approval or disapproval. The decrepit old men may very well be withering into truth as they lament the passing of all things beautiful.[5]

Neither ambiguous nor paradoxical is the aging Yeats's attitude toward the unpleasant reality of the passing of beautiful things, especially when they are emblematic of a great culture on the wane. One of his angriest confrontations with time—which "always plays with loaded dice"—is embodied in "In Memory of Eva Gore-Booth and Con Markiewicz" (1927), a dialectically structured poem revealing a much more sophisticated attitude than earlier poems of related theme. Sharing Yeats's meditation on the destructiveness of time, we follow his thesis beyond denunciation to the destruction of time itself. The poem memorializes not only the youthful innocence and beauty of the Gore-Booth sisters (revolutionaries now turned "withered old and skeleton gaunt" like their politics) and the gentle society that they adorned, but recalls as well the idealistic youth of the poet and his now hollow dream of order. All coherence gone, emblems of stability and grace (silk kimonos, gazelle, Georgian mansion) give way to Utopian pipedreams and degrading conspiracy. Yeats balances tenderness and indignation until his desertion amidst the colossal wreck of all that the past stood for becomes too painful to bear:

> *The innocent and the beautiful*
> *Have no enemy but time;*
> *Arise and bid me strike a match*
> *And strike another till time catch;*
> *Should the conflagration climb,*
> *Run till all the sages know.*
> *We the great gazebo built,*
> *They convicted us of guilt;*
> *Bid me strike a match and blow.*[6]

The striking image of the burning of time was not new to Yeats's poetry—only its violent aspect. In "He Tells of the Perfect Beauty" (written 1895), we find, in a peaceful context, the hyperbole of time being burned by a God sympathetic to love. Similarly, in the first version of "The Shadowy Waters" (published 1900), Forgael speaks of "the soft fire/That shall burn time when times have ebbed away," and later in the poem we find a related metaphor of time "drowned in odour-laden winds/And druid moons, and murmuring of boughs."[7] But with the passing of years, as Yeats's verse grew in drive and depth, so too the hardness and complexity of his attitude toward the problem of time. The basic orientation, however, remained constant for many years.

The controlled but nonetheless violent image of the closing lines of his elegy on the Gore-Booth sisters is matched in boldness and belligerence by the ending of "The Lamentation of the Old Pensioner." Study of this radically rewritten poem (1925) and its earlier version (1890) affords us a good opportunity to observe Yeats's developing concern for the problem of time and old age.

The source of the poem is a sketch of George Russell published in *The Celtic Twilight* (1893). Yeats recounts one of AE's experiences with an old peasant, who, upset because his fading life had left him bereft of achievement and hope, was "wandering in his mind with prolonged sorrow": "Once he burst out with, 'God possesses the heavens—God possesses the heavens—but He covets the world'; and once he lamented that his old neighbours were gone, and that all had forgotten him: they used to draw a chair to the fire for him in every cabin, and now they said, 'Who is that old fellow there?' 'The fret' (Irish for doom) 'is over me,' he repeated, and then went on to talk once more of God and Heaven."[8]

In the 15 November 1890 issue of the *Scots Observer* Yeats published "The Old Pensioner," which he described in notes to the early editions of his poems as "little more than a translation into verse of the very words of an old Wicklow peasant":

> *I had a chair at every hearth,*
> *When no one turned to see*
> *With "Look at that old fellow there;*
> *And who may he be?"*
> *And therefore do I wander on,*
> *And the fret is on me.*
>
> *The road-side trees keep murmuring—*
> *Ah, wherefore murmur ye*
> *As in the old days long gone by,*
> *Green oak and poplar tree!*
> *The well-known faces are all gone,*
> *And the fret is on me.*

Rewritten for the 1925 edition of *Early Poems and Stories*, the poem now reads:

Although I shelter from the rain
Under a broken tree
My chair was nearest to the fire
In every company
That talked of love and politics,
Ere Time transfigured me.

Though lads are making pikes again
For some conspiracy,
And crazy rascals rage their fill
At human tyranny,
My contemplations are of Time
That has transfigured me.

There's not a woman turns her face
Upon a broken tree,
And yet the beauties that I loved
Are in my memory;
I spit into the face of Time
That has transfigured me.

As is evident, Yeats has written virtually a new poem. A poignant experience not far removed from melancholy nostalgia has been changed utterly into a carefully plotted denunciation of time and mutability. Although Yeats made revisions in many of his early poems, he rewrote very few, and thus it is all the more significant that at the age of sixty he turned his attention to this particular piece of juvenilia. Whereas the original version confessedly is not much more than a poetic analogue of AE's story, the new version uses the story only as a basis for the delineation of an attitude and for the passing of judgment. In this respect, the entirely new second stanza serves an important purpose: by expanding the compass of the pensioner's contemplation, it relates his experience to the recurrences of the historical process.

In the earlier version the speaker, doomed by age to solitude, is reduced merely to wistful remembrance; in the new version, where he apprehends his plight cosmologically, he not only ascribes causality to "Time," but also sees himself metamorphosed by its blind operation. Yeats's selection of the verb *transfigure* is important, for the word not only means change of form or appearance, i.e., metamorphosis, but also denotes the exaltation and glorification resulting from such change. Its use here, then, is paradoxical and ironic: the speaker has been devastated and reduced by time; yet time's workings have illumined his being and granted him heightened vision.[9] Hence, where formerly he had confronted his painful destiny by wandering, he is now able to perform an assertive (albeit futile) gesture of defiance.[10] Defiance and rage, at once heroic and futile, are the dominant notes of most of the poetry of Yeats's last years.

Similarly, when we consider the transformation of the murmuring roadside "green" oaks and poplars to a mute and solitary "broken tree" (symbolic both of the imperfect shelter afforded the old man in his old age, and of old age itself), we are struck by the far wider implications of the later version: not only has a local and personal experience been made more intense, more concrete, but it has been given universal dimension and public import as well.

"The Lamentation of the Old Pensioner" prefigures future accomplishments, for the poem embodies very many of the significant features of Yeats's last poems. Among others we may note the stark, desolate, and economically sketched imagery of the natural scene, and the correspondingly conceived speaker; the transcendental view of public affairs and of the gyrations of history; a sense of impending disaster coupled with scorn for those who become mired in futile countermeasures; the memory of friends and loves long departed; the conflict between sexual incapacity and desire; and the perspective of "lust and rage" which fuses them all into unified experience and expression.

Anxious to transcend all immensities of the "Grey Truth" which he felt was rapidly overwhelming the nineteenth century, Yeats early identified himself with Hermetic doctrine and symbolist practice. In a now famous autobiographical statement he declared: "I am very religious, and deprived by Huxley and Tyndall, whom I detested, of the simple-minded religion of my childhood. I had made a new religion, almost an infallible Church of poetic tradition, of a fardel of stories, and of personages, and of emotions. . . . I wished for a world where I could discover all this tradition perpetually. . . ."[11] As a disciple of the Rosy Cross, Yeats not only perceived correspondences between the sundered worlds of heaven and earth, but (in the other aspect of the symbol) saw beauty and spirit nailed to the tree of time and matter. Like other transcendentalists before him, he recognized

> . . . *two laws discrete,*
> *Not reconciled,* —
> *Law for man, and law for thing,*

and similarly concluded that

> *The last builds town and fleet,*
> *But it runs wild,*
> *And doth the man unking.*[12]

After announcing that "The woods of Arcady are dead," the speaker of one of Yeats's earliest poems, "The Song of the Happy Shepherd," vows to attune himself to verities accessible to the still faithful heart of those who keep the trust of happier generations and their satisfying scheme of order. In the opening lines he contrasts the lost Arcadian land of joyful dreams and heroic deeds to the "idle story" of his own materialistic world aimlessly dancing to the "cracked tune" of change and whirl now sung by the dreary god of time. Because "there is no truth/Saving in thine own heart," and because all else proves weak or untrue, he preaches solipsistic introspection and commends to the "sick children of the world" a womblike, "twisted, echo-harbouring" sea shell—truly a classic image of subjective withdrawal, and of the work of art into which the unreconstructed artist withdraws as he prosecutes his underground mission. Urging that we tell our cares to the lips of this comforting chamber, he asserts that its "melodious guile" will transform our "fretful words" into agreeable artistic constructs because "words alone are certain good."

Happily lost in the mists of Celtic twilight and the pristine imagery of Pre-Raphaelite vision, Yeats's shepherd conjures forth daffodils and lilies, and dedicates his "songs of old earth's dreamy youth" to the resuscitation of some "hapless faun,/Buried under the sleepy ground." Unable, perhaps, to convince completely, Yeats wisely turns to the magic of words and the power of positive incantation. At the end, he consummates the melodious beguilement of the reader by enveloping him in a swirl of dream dust. Because the earth has passed from divine order to positive science and thus no longer can dream, it is we who, aided by "poppies on the brow," must do so. It is revealing that in its original context, as an epilogue to *The Island of Statues* and *The Seeker* (1885), the shepherd's song praises the choice of men who, having been brought back to life from enchantment into statues, preferred to live enisled in Arcady rather than return to the world.

Thus revolting against the crass concerns of a culture hostile to imagination and indifferent to heroism, Yeats urges escape from the tedium of time and the "Grey Truth" of its latest legacy. Along with its concomitant, "denunciation of old age," the theme of escape dominates many of his poems, especially those written before the turn of the century. Down to the old man of "Sailing to Byzantium," the time-wearied protagonists of these poems become fugitives from the distressing circumstances of their unfulfilled lives. True romantics, with Keats and his kin they yearn to "fade away into the forest dim," far from "the weariness, the fever, and the fret/Here, where men sit and hear each other groan."

In *The Wanderings of Oisin,* using myth and symbol as instruments of escape, Yeats sends his frustrated hero across inviting seas to magic islands representing "three incompatible things which man is always seeking—infinite feeling, infinite battle, infinite repose."[13] Oisin heeds the call of Niamh, his fairy abductor, and rides to realms devoid of "burial mounds," where time is a tune and innocence and faith remain forever. "We rode out from the human lands," Oisin declares, but though he denounced old age and "mocked at Time and Fate and Chance," emblems of the world he left behind—"O wandering Oisin, the strength of the bell-branch is naught,/For there moves alive in your fingers the fluttering sadness of earth"—betook him home from the islands and eventually left him a dying old man "sick with years," "bent, and bald, and blind,/With a heavy heart and a wandering mind."

Echoes of *The Wanderings of Oisin* abound throughout many of Yeats's earliest poems, such as "Love Song" (subtitled "From the Gaelic"), published in *Poems and Ballads of Young Ireland* (1888) but never included elsewhere.[14] In "The Hosting of the Sidhe," Niamh calls "Away, come away:/Empty your heart of its mortal dream," while in "Into the Twilight" (first published at the end of *The Celtic Twilight* as though it were an epilogue) the speaker contrasts "mother Eire," eternally young, with a weary modern mortal ("Out-worn heart, in a time out-worn") and bids him "come clear of the nets of wrong and right" to a refuge where "God stands winding His lonely horn,/And time and the world are ever in flight."

CONTEMPLATIONS OF TIME   15

Oisin is but the first of Yeats's heroes to journey across water to idyllic, time-free haunts. In "The Stolen Child" we discover a call very similar to Niamh's in the summons that would spirit away the human child from the press of life's anguish, "For the world's more full of weeping" than he can now hope to understand. And because the world is more full of weeping than confused youth can fathom, in "A Faery Song" the ancient and gay people of fairyland offer Diarmuid and Grania, sleeping newlyweds, "rest far from men."

Especially in the early versions of "The Indian to His Love," a much revised poem, the familiar summons is again sounded unmistakably. In the original version (1886), the speaker, after announcing that "Our isle awaits us," envisions Arcadian bliss far removed from "all earth's feverish lands":

> There dreary Time lets fall his sickle
> And Life the sandals of her fleetness,
> And sleek young Joy is no more fickle,
> And Love is kindly and deceitless,
> And life is over save the murmur and the sweetness.[15]

Actual occurrences in Yeats's life are responsible for the conception of two early poems centered on this escape theme, and both of them—"The Lake Isle of Innisfree" and "The White Birds"—characteristically involve flight over water.

In the former, echoing the resolve of the Prodigal Son ("I will arise and go to seek my father. . . ."), Yeats yearns for the consolations of home. In "The Trembling of the Veil" he describes how he came to write the poem. Recalling his lonely days in London, he recounts how, "walking through Fleet Street very homesick," he was reminded of lake water by the sight of a little ball balanced on a jet of water emanating from a fountain in a shop window.[16] He relates much the same experience in his novel, *John Sherman*, where ball and jet cause the hero to remember not only the homespun girl he left behind in Ireland, but also "an old day-dream" concerning "a little islet called Inniscrewin": "Oft when life and its difficulties had seemed to him like the lessons of some older boy given to a younger by mistake, it had seemed good to dream of going away to that islet and building a wooden hut there and burning a few years out, rowing to and fro, fishing, or lying on the island slopes by day, and listening at night to the ripple of the water and the quivering of the bushes—full always of unknown creatures—and going out at morning to see the island's edge marked by the feet of birds."[17] In a letter to Katharine Tynan he makes his intention even more explicit: "There is a beautiful Island of Innisfree in Lough Gill, Sligo. A little rocky Island with a legended past. In my story I make one of the characters whenever he is in trouble long to go away and live alone on that Island—an old daydream of my own. Thinking over his feelings I made these verses about them. . . ."[18]

During the summer of 1891 Yeats asked Maud Gonne to marry him but was refused because she wanted a man of action, someone committed to the here and now.[19] The day after her refusal they walked on the cliffs at Howth where they saw two seagulls appear and then quickly fly out to sea. Maud casually remarked that if she could become a bird she would choose the seagull, whereupon Yeats sent her three days later a copy of "The White Birds," a poem presumably occasioned by her remark.[20] "Haunted by numberless islands," the ardent speaker yearns to be a white bird and join his beloved in flying from "Time" and "Sorrow." In notes appended to the poem in early editions of his works, Yeats drew an analogy between the carefree birds of this poem and the snow-white birds of fairyland, and similarly identified the "Danaan shore" with Tir-nan-oge, fairyland.

Because the here and now is no country for this dreamy young man, he hypothesizes an Arcadian existence ironically analogous to the much more complex but equally time-free realm of the golden bird of "Sailing to Byzantium." In a similar (but more domestic) mood, the speaker of another early poem, celebrating the "shy one of my heart," announces that "To an isle in the water/With her I would fly."[21] In all, many poems of Yeats's apprenticeship show that enroute to Byzantium and its sophisticated splendors, young Yeats was haunted by innocent dreams of Arcadian islands promising release from "Time" and its attendant "Sorrow." In an early story, an old man on the eve of his death sums it up: "I have sought through all my life to find the secret of life. I was not happy in my youth, for I knew that it would pass; and I was not happy in my manhood, for I knew that age was coming; and so I gave myself, in youth and manhood and age, to the search for the Great Secret. . . . I gave myself to magic . . . that I might bring the gods and the Men of Faery to my side. . . . To-morrow . . . I will go away to a southern land

and build myself a palace of white marble amid orange-trees, and gather the brave and the beautiful about me, and enter into the eternal kingdom of my youth."[22]

If late in life, looking back over his poetic achievement he could discern but a single dominant theme, likewise in his youth he was able to perceive that theme for what it actually was and thus pass judgment on it. The not yet twenty-three-year-old dreamer confessed: "I have much improved 'Mosada' by polishing the verse here and there. I have noticed some things about my poetry I did not know before, in this process of correction; for instance, that it is almost all a flight into fairyland from the real world, and a summons to that flight. The Chorus to the 'Stolen Child' sums it up—that it is not the poetry of insight and knowledge, but of longing and complaint—the cry of the heart against necessity. I hope someday to alter that and write poetry of insight and knowledge."[23] Nearly all of Yeats's poetry may very profitably be studied in the light of this statement.

The onset of old age pushed Yeats deeper into "longing and complaint," but it also enabled him to probe into profounder areas of awareness. A rich poem in its own right, "The Tower" deserves our attention here because it embodies one of Yeats's most sustained meditations on old age and thus serves as a kind of prologue to "Sailing to Byzantium," his last and most accomplished "cry of the heart against necessity."

Thoor Ballylee, Yeats's storm-battered Anglo-Norman tower, stands not far from once ceremonious Coole and its now desecrated "Seven Woods." In its stark and lonely aspect, this "powerful emblem" set up "In mockery of a time/Half dead at the top" symbolizes the pride and isolation of the introspective seeker of hidden truth, while its winding "ancestral stair," recalling the gyres of time, declares the seeker's affinity with figures from an arrogant and immoderate past. Here Yeats came to live in 1919, and from here, a few years later, he wrote to a friend: "I am tired and in a rage at being old. I am all I ever was and much more but an enemy has bound me and twisted me so I can plan and think as I never could, but no longer achieve all I plan and think."[24]

This certainly is the predominant concern of "The Tower,"

whose focus is the conflict between power and capacity. "Decrepit age" tied to the speaker's body as though to the tail of a dog not only troubles him but also burdens him with a maddening "absurdity." Never had this imagination been more "Excited, passionate, fantastical," nor his "ear and eye" so acutely eager. (In keeping with the theme, ear and eye imagery predominates. See also lines 13, 17, 31, 44, 49, 52, 75, 94, 101, 110, 140, and 190.) Accordingly, summoning forth images "in the Great Memory stored," he would question all who have come to the tower during its fabled, violent past and ask if they, too, raged against crippling age. Most notable of all who are summoned is Yeats's picturesque creation of years back, frenzied Hanrahan the Red. Dismissing all, Yeats would keep this "old lecher with a love on every wind" because he seeks "all his mighty memories," recollections of which are to beget many poems of the next decade, for Hanrahan is a prototype of numerous *personae* in *Last Poems* —frenzied seers, roaring tinkers, and other "wild old wicked men." But that is a long way off. Now, choosing Plato and Plotinus for friends, Yeats hopes to surmount the absurdity of his condition by consorting with sages emblematic of those masters toward whose "learned school" he would eagerly set sail a year or two later.

"I will go now," an appropriate echo of the opening line of "The Lake Isle of Innisfree," appears very early in the prose fragment from which, according to Jon Stallworthy and Mrs. Yeats, "Sailing to Byzantium" (1926–1927) finally grew.[25] In this justly celebrated poem, a monument to the magnificence of the romantic imagination and its exaltation of art and artist, Yeats once again assumes his by now classic posture of flight. "Salmon-falls" and other sights and sounds of the phenomenal world, though poignantly recalled, serve only to accent all the more his own mortal taint.[26] The values of this world teeming and brimming over with life he declares to be evanescent, not only because all living things must pass through inevitable cycles of generation and corruption, but also because (the suggestion seems sure) such a world precludes the full participation of the speaker.

Counterpointing the contemplative song that the soul must sing to the "sensual music" spawned in a world of endless cycles of birth, decay, and death, Yeats would travel the purgatorial way to salvation and apotheosis. "Sick with desire" he desires to yearn no more and thus spurns life for a state of artificial transcendency. Transmuted into a golden bird he would contemplate all eternity from his static perch in the "Eternal Now."[27] Here, in stasis at the still point of the turning world, he would sing of his escape from time.

Though now his art is sure and his poetry commensurately full of insight and knowledge, the fact of his flight is incontrovertible: echoes of the early poems resound as we once again discover "longing and complaint—the cry of the heart against necessity."[28] As he had written in 1922, in "Meditations in Time of Civil War," "Only an aching heart/Conceives a changeless work of art." This confession not only confirms the tragic basis of artistic creation, but reveals significant commentary on Yeats's own development as well, for only a heart much beset by the burden of time would will to exchange life for chirping timelessness. Yeats's great achievement here, however, lies in his exposition of the artist's will to transcend phenomenal limitations, and in the symbolic identification of creator and created. From another aspect, this exquisite lyric extolling that which is exquisitely wrought presents us with but another denunciation of "Old Age and Time." Poems of "insight," wise because of their celebration of all tatters of mortal dress, were still to be written.

CHAPTER TWO ✳ THE LIVING WORLD

IT IS NOT ETERNITY itself that the suffering speaker of "Sailing to Byzantium" craves; neither oblivion, *nirvana*, nor *nada*, but a tangible analogue of it. When he prays for union with "the artifice of eternity," we understand that he is here pleading not for the real thing but for some imitation, or approximation. But where eternity is concerned, how satisfying is a semblance? Even at the height of his aged speaker's transcendental triumph, Yeats was perhaps aware of this ambiguity. The speaker's moving sketch of the world he was leaving behind, his head cocked back, as it were, as he sailed toward the holy fire of stasis, adds to the hypothesis that the poem contains the germ of its counterstatement.

Further, *artifice* is a curious word: almost every important term used to establish its denotation contains an essential ambiguity; to define the word we are forced to use terms whose multiple connotations are at great variance. *Artifice* means "artful or skillful contrivance": this is and is not pejorative. Recognition of more recent usage, moreover, may be noted in the succeeding entry: "Crafty device; trickery." Again: "An artful stratagem or trick." Looking up artful (for example) we find: "Craftily designed; ingeniously deceptive," and "cunning . . . crafty."[1] And so on. Likewise, the "holy fire," here symbolic of divine purgation and the resultant state of beatitude, may be similarly regarded, for the "holy fire" characteristic of Byzantine mosaic art was achieved by skillfully deploying irregular bits of glass so as to reflect light in great concentration along strategic areas of the wall, thereby creating the illusion of extreme luminescence. To be sure, "artifice of eternity" presents us primarily with a "supreme fiction" in Wallace Stevens's sense of the term; at the same time, however, we are reminded that this particular supreme fiction, Platonic or otherwise, is but a "royal lie" passed on to prospective citizens of Yeats's republic of the disembodied mind.

The careful reader of "Sailing to Byzantium" detects reservation and hesitation, as he does with many other of Yeats's seemingly declarative poems. For all its often bold and convincing assertiveness, Yeats's verse is frequently freighted with vacillation, compromise, and doubt. In "To the Rose upon the Rood of Time," for example, we find a situation strikingly similar to that in "Sailing to Byzantium." Invoking the Rose, that proud, sad emblem of "eternal beauty," Yeats announces that he would sing of Ireland and of the Rose itself. The first stanza ends with a plea for the Rose to "Come near," but in the immediately succeeding lines, however, we find him hedging:

> Come near, come near, come near—Ah, leave me still
> A little space for the rose-breath to fill!
> Lest I no more hear common things that crave;
> The weak worm hiding down in its small cave,
> The field-mouse running by me in the grass,
> And heavy mortal hopes that toil and pass. . . .

Just as the eternity occupied by the sages of Byzantium is—in W. Y. Tindall's term—"provisional,"[2] so also here the poet's desired locus lies somewhere between the passing and the lasting. Similarly, in "Ribh at the Tomb of Baile and Aillinn" we discover that mystic circles are perceived imperfectly even by aged eyes "made aquiline" by diet and prayer. Though it illumines the hermit's "holy book," the ring of light generated by copulating angels overhead is "somewhat broken by the leaves"—time's shadow, as it were, intruding upon emanations from eternity.[3] Finally, as though commenting on his timeless golden bird, Yeats said that J. W. Dunne's "infinite observer" of *An Experiment with Time* "happens to touch on a very difficult problem, one I have been a good deal bothered by. If I could know all the past

and all the future and see it as a single instant I would still be
conditioned, limited, by the form of that past and the form of
that future, I would not be infinite."⁴

Though all roads may have led Yeats to Byzantium, they beck-
oned beyond. For all the glory of their changeless condition,
neither starlit dome nor moon-embittered bird could scorn too
long all that man lives and stands for. One of the most striking
features of the poetry of Yeats's full maturity is an ever-increasing
insistence not only on his own humanity but on an acceptance
of the full range of experience as well. Though he discovered
that they were not to be transcended, he succeeded in transfiguring "the fury and the mire of human veins" into impassioned
complexities of wonder and affirmation. Learning from his vision
of wholeness that great things blossom where "the body is not
bruised to pleasure soul," Yeats ultimately came to celebrate the
rich confusion of life.

"A Dialogue of Self and Soul," written very shortly after
"Sailing to Byzantium," presents the conflicting claims of passive
contemplation and passionate commitment.⁵ Preaching disem-
bodiment of mind, the Soul urges ascent to Byzantine "breathless
starlit air," and promises deliverance "from the crime of death
and birth." The Self, however, rejecting such disengagement,
clings to an ancient sword covered by "flowering, silken, old
embroidery, torn/From some court-lady's dress," and affirms that
this covering "Can, tattered, still protect, faded adorn." To Olivia
Shakespear Yeats wrote, "I make my Japanese sword and its silk
covering my symbol of life"⁶—and indeed he did, for the sword,
"emblematic of love and war," also symbolizes the "still razor-
keen" poet proudly covered and adorned by every tatter of his
mortal dress.

Sword and sheath of "heart's purple" he then declares to be
"emblems of the day" against the tower of night, and claims "as
by a soldier's right/A charter to commit the crime once more."
On the defensive throughout the give and take of part one, in
part two the Self rises to peroration as he holds the stage all
alone:

> A living man is blind and drinks his drop.
> What matter if the ditches are impure?
> What matter if I live at all once more?

·   ·   ·

I am content to live it all again
And yet again, if it be life to pitch
Into the frog-spawn of a blind man's ditch,
A blind man battering blind men;

     .   .   .

I am content to follow to its source
Every event in action or in thought;
Measure the lot; forgive myself the lot!
When such as I cast out remorse
So great a sweetness flows into the breast
We must laugh and we must sing,
We are blest by everything,
Everything we look upon is blest.

"A Dialogue of Self and Soul" is a pivotal poem, a work interrupted by illness and resumed after Yeats had faced in reality the release that heretofore he had conjured in his imagination and embodied in beguiling artifacts. After facing the very real possibility of death and whatever journey lay beyond, Yeats the man who knew that he could and would die, that is to say, Yeats the man of flesh and bone (*carne y hueso*, Unamuno's term), turned to sing an impassioned response to his exquisitely inhuman golden bird. Exquisite but inhuman nonetheless, the bird of Byzantine pose had perched aloft and apart from the generality of men and the core of their human involvements. Its song, timeless, simultaneously encompassed all time and thus not the time given to existential man, to this man and that man—"the unfinished man and his pain"—to play out the drama of his mortality, however absurd and clumsy the circumstances. The philosopher, according to Plato, is always pursuing death because death cuts the shackles that fetter distracting body to better-deserving soul; but existential man, "the free man," as Unamuno interprets Spinoza, "thinks of nothing less than of death, and his wisdom consists in meditating not on death but on life." Further, the golden bird was time-free, but time-free is history-free, and yet it is in history, in historical process, that man's life is set—in history that the "ditches" of the blind and battered are located, that men, under sentence of death but indefinitely reprieved, reach out to one another for the consolations of touch and the satisfactions of community. As for Sisyphus, so for the Self: one must imagine them happy.

"Apropos of much," Yeats wrote to his friend and biographer Joseph Hone, perhaps while composing this poem, "much of the confusion of modern philosophy, perhaps the whole realism versus idealism quarrel," is the result of our renunciation of "the ancient hierarchy of beings from man up to the One." Though all creatures are limited, he continues, each complements another in such a way as to make possible a unitive vision of all creation: "What I do not see but may see or have seen, is perceived by another being. I remember what he forgets, he remembers what I forget. We are in the midst of life and there is nothing but life."[7]

To be "in the midst of life" entailed acceptance of "contraries." "Without Contraries there is no progression," Yeats was fond of quoting from Blake's *The Marriage of Heaven and Hell*; and his own progress may be plotted in terms of his effort to establish equilibrium between contending forces of "Attraction and Repulsion, Reason and Energy, Love and Hate." Because wholeness, like life, is a composite of opposing but complementary forces, body and soul, Yeats came to affirm, must not be separated. Between 1929 and 1931, when he composed *Words for Music Perhaps*, Yeats the swordsman was to fight off physical death as he wrote poems directed toward the attainment of a more satisfactory balance between "Self" and "Soul."

Begun a few months before his near-fatal attack of Malta fever in December 1929, and continued during the following year and a half, these songs of "poetical rebirth"[8] comprising the *Words for Music Perhaps* sequence explore impure ditches as mysterious as the lyrics themselves. "Ill and yet full of desire"—the poems were bred by "sexual abstinence," he told Mrs. Shakespear[9]— Yeats yearned for "desecration and the lover's night."[10] Heart, body, self—these are the claims pressed by Crazy Jane and Old Tom as they celebrate nature and nature's processes.

Crazy Jane's running battle with the Bishop epitomizes Yeats's new state of existential awareness. "More or less founded upon an old woman who lives in a little cottage near Gort," this hardy peasant brings "epic magnificence" to her ferocious quarrels against asceticism and abnegation. As though armed with all seventy of Blake's hellish proverbs and more of her own, "she is the local satirist and a really terrible one."[11] "I approve of her," Yeats wrote.[12]

In "Crazy Jane and the Bishop" we learn that the "solid"

Bishop, "an old book in his fist," long ago had banished Jane's "coxcomb" lover because they "lived like beast and beast."[13] Maddened Jane's curses, however, disclose a reversal of values and attributes. At "midnight upon the stroke" it becomes clear that

> *The Bishop has a skin, God knows,*
> *Wrinkled like the foot of a goose,*
> (All find safety in the tomb.)
> *Nor can he hide in holy black*
> *The Heron's hunch upon his back*
> *But a birch-tree stood my Jack:*
> The solid man and the coxcomb.

Although the terminal refrain remains constant throughout, its use in the last two stanzas reveals Jack as upstanding, the Bishop as educated fool. In this respect the birch-tree metaphor is central to and characteristic of Jane's transforming metaphysic. Jack is presented in terms of an image of sexuality, a phallus, which the Bishop (in a later poem) would decry as "foul." Yet the birch tree, in its proud and tall whiteness, also suggests purity and the grandeur of a solidly-rooted structure. And the "blasted oak," at first suggestive of "witchcraft's favorite tree,"[14] now represents not only imperfect shelter for old age, but also a code of values more archetypal and therefore more elemental and "solid" than that of the cruel Bishop and his unrenewed, renunciatory church.

The burden to "Crazy Jane Grown Old Looks at the Dancers" declares that "*Love is like the lion's tooth*"—stark, terrifying, consuming, but also noble, clean, and bare. This beauty, built of wholeness, demands wholeness. Thus in "Crazy Jane on the Day of Judgment" we learn that

> "*Love is all*
> *Unsatisfied*
> *That cannot take the whole*
> *Body and soul*";
> And that is what Jane said.

As for love, so for life. In "Crazy Jane Talks with the Bishop," to the latter's charge that henceforth she "Live in a heavenly mansion,/Not in some foul sty," Jane argues the concomitance of seemingly disparate elements: "Fair and foul are near of kin,/ And fair needs foul," she cries. Such a paradoxical truth, we learn, issues from the marvelously complex nature of man, his "bodily lowliness" and his "heart's pride."[15] "What matter if the ditches are impure?" the Self had cried during its great affirmation, and here the cry is picked up in Jane's homely conclusion:

> *"A woman can be proud and stiff*
> *When on love intent;*
> *But Love has pitched his mansion in*
> *The place of excrement;*
> *For nothing can be sole or whole*
> *That has not been rent."*

In addition to recalling Yeats's recent illnesses, the last two lines forcefully posit conditions necessary for "Unity of Being." Moreover, in reading these lines we should keep in mind Donald Stauffer's ingenious notice of a "purposeful" ambiguity: *sole* and *whole*, he observes, "might as well be written" *soul* and *hole*. We have here more evidence not only of "Yeats's sense of necessary conflict and necessary wholeness,"[16] but also—I would add—of his belief, with Blake, that until "the notion that man has a body distinct from his soul is . . . expunged," "the doors of perception" can never be "cleansed."[17]

"Cruachan's windy plain," though the scene of an ecstatic dance, is a long way off from timeless Byzantium and its "breathless" air. In "the Holy Land of Ireland," Yeats once remarked, Irish monks avowed Christ to be "the most beautiful of men," and an Irish saint sang, "There is one among the beasts that is perfect, one among the fish, one perfect among men."[18] Hence, in "The Dancer at Cruachan and Cro-Patrick" the speaker identifies divinity with perfection of form, but does not do so disdainfully in scorn of living things. Quite the contrary, for the saintly dancer perning in adoration of such an *ens perfectissimum* accepts and rejoices in the ultimate unity of all creation. Proclaiming perfection and peace, the grateful dancer envisions all creation "Acclaiming, proclaiming, declaiming Him."

"Men come, men go," Crazy Jane averred, but *"All things remain in God."*[19] Likewise, this is the sustaining conviction of Jane's kinsman, "old Tom the lunatic," who echoes the cry in the face of terror and death. Because he sees through mutability to an awesome pattern of permanence beyond, his testament is charged with vigorous acceptance and undying faith:

> *"Whatever stands in field or flood,*
> *Bird, beast, fish or man,*
> *Mare or stallion, cock or hen,*
> *Stands in God's unchanging eye*
> *In all the vigour of its blood;*
> *In that faith I live or die."*

The final line is especially telling because it is drawn from the refrain of François Villon's *"Ballade que Villon feist a la requeste de sa mere pour prier Nostre Dame"*: *"En ceste foy je vueil vivre et mourir."* Old Tom is a fit analogue of Villon's speaker, who, meditating upon the terrors faced by some sorely tried souls, confesses a simple, pious, and firm faith in the comforting pattern of God's mercy.[20]

Though *The Winding Stair* begins with the assertion that innocence and beauty "have no enemy but time" ("In Memory of Eva Gore-Booth and Con Markiewicz" is the opening poem), and throughout proceeds to demonstrate this unalterable law, it closes not with foolhardy conflagration—the burning of time itself—but with the impassioned song of inflamed fools who with Blake cry, "Everything that lives is holy, life delights in life."[21] And like "that William Blake," Yeats asserts ancient truth against the partial visions of false orthodoxies. Speaking through Crazy Jane and loony Tom, like Blake he spreads "the voice of the devil" throughout the land:

All Bibles or sacred codes have been the causes of the following Errors:

1. That Man has two real existing principles: Viz: a Body & a Soul.

2. That Energy, call'd Evil, is alone from the Body; & that Reason, call'd Good, is alone from the Soul.

3. That God will torment Man in Eternity for following his Energies.

But the following Contraries to these are True:

1. Man has no Body distinct from his Soul; for that call'd Body is a portion of Soul discern'd by the five Senses; the chief inlets of Soul in this age.

2. Energy is the only life, and is from the Body; and Reason is the bound or outward circumference of Energy.

3. Energy is Eternal Delight.[22]

While Jane and Tom discover spirituality in all material things, tonsured Ribh, a singer of supernatural songs, proclaims the marriage of heaven and earth, and finds materiality in the world of spirit:

> Natural and supernatural with the self-same
>   ring are wed.
> As man, as beast, as an ephemeral fly begets,
>   Godhead begets Godhead,
> For things below are copies, the Great Smaragdine
>   Tablet said.[23]

Delighting in eternal energy, Ribh reads his sacred book by the glow of copulating angels;[24] and preferring an older theology, he declares that all trinities, because analogues of the natural world, must reflect its composition by uniting man, woman, and child. Thus his denunciation of Patrick, a newcomer "crazed" by "An abstract Greek absurdity" that denies the plain truth of "all natural or supernatural stories."[25]

Because the way of God "passes human wit," Ribh learns to "study hatred with great diligence." His "jealous" soul, freed from "terror and deception," by discovering "impurities" can surmount the agonies of a fallen world and fear no more. Man, by his deceiving pride and his essential imperfection, vainly promotes the imperfect gods conceived in his limited intellect; but the "fool," knowing that the way down is also the way out, attains to mystic wisdom and the sight of God.[26]

Thus embattled "in the midst of life" because "there is nothing but life," Yeats discovered that neither as a man nor as an artist could he work for wholeness of vision, harmony of thought, and radiance of essence until he had been diverted from "the way of the bird" downward "to the market carts" where "all is simplified and solidified again."[27]

We have seen in "Sailing to Byzantium" how Yeats, vexed into flight by a nightmare of mortality, created through his art a type of eternity amenable to the claims of his questing soul. This poem, according to Stephen Dedalus's description of "lyric," reveals its creator presenting "his image in immediate relation to himself." Further, following Stephen, we may add that here truly "the esthetic urge . . . is life purified in and reprojected from the human imagination."[28] It is important to note, however, that this poem embodies important parallel achievements. Certainly, it affords one of the most compelling demonstrations of the power of the aesthetic urge. In this connection, the golden bird singing in and of eternity represents not only a satisfying form for the reincarnation of the suffering poet, but exemplifies as well the process by which art may be created; for in the pattern of journey, prayer, purgation, and apotheosis, we see an analogue for the process whereby the dedicated artist transmutes the chaos of finite experience into ordered and eternal imaginative worlds. Consummating "the mystery of esthetic," Yeats echoes the words of another fabulous artificer: "O! In the virgin womb of the imagination the word was made flesh."[29]

Few would question that Yeats was seriously dedicated to his art. So serious was this dedication that for over fifty years the man and the poet are identified in recurrent interaction. Yeats's involvement with his work was so intense and thorough that most of the time it is difficult for us to disentangle the poet himself from the masks and voices of his poems: dancer and dance often whirl as one.[30] Because Yeats was a man given to confess all, almost everything within the compass of his experience eventually found its way into his prodigious writings; in turn, these writings returned, as it were, to reshape his past and future life. If ever that abused phrase "the life of art" had meaning for anyone, certainly it had for Yeats, who throughout his life directed all his resources toward the consuming task of perfecting his work.

He dedicated himself to the perfection of his work with virtually a vengeance. In "The Choice" he proposes a hard antinomy between the mutually exclusive callings of spiritual refinement and unstinting artistic devotion. Man's intellect, he notes, is compelled to choose between "Perfection of the life, or of the work," and if it selects the latter it must abandon all hope of attaining a "heavenly mansion." Because Yeats's choice commits him to the raging dark of an imperfect world, louder sing he must if through that choice his world is to provide substance for well-wrought work. "He must," as John Unterecker has phrased it, "for the sake of his work, live life to the hilt."[31] Deliberate or otherwise, Unterecker's pun is pregnant, for as Yeats wrote to Olivia Shakespear (shortly after composing the poem) concerning the work of a lifetime, "the swordsman throughout repudiates the saint, but not without vacillation." "Is that perhaps the sole theme" of all his work, he wondered, "Usheen and Patrick—'so get you gone Von Hügel though with blessings on your head'?"[32]

Straddling the two realms of spirit and matter, but no longer solidly set like the "great Amphibium" of 1635, the artist often finds himself vacillating between the "divided and distinguished worlds" of eternity and time.[33] "Vacillation," that ensemble of double visions, is basically—for all its complexity—a reorchestration of themes familiar to readers of "A Dialogue of Self and Soul" and "The Choice." Running his course between the "extremities" implicit in "Perfection of the life, or of the work," by the end of the poem Yeats takes his stand with the claims of his art and the passions that make it possible. His choice is not surprising. "Man is in love and loves what vanishes," he had written a decade earlier, "What more is there to say?"[34] Though bitterly aware that monuments of sword and song are transitory, that "all things pass away," he could not now forsake the living sounds of the dying generations.[35] Though the mute simplicity of heavenly fire promised release and salvation, it precluded his further functioning as a creative artist:

> The Soul. *Seek out reality, leave things that seem.*
> The Heart. *What, be a singer born and lack a theme?*
> The Soul. *Isaiah's coal, what more can man desire?*
> The Heart. *Struck dumb in the simplicity of fire!*[36]
> The Soul. *Look on that fire, salvation walks within.*
> The Heart. *What theme had Homer but original sin?*[37]

Similarly, in the last section (where, accepting miracles and honoring sanctity, he blesses but dismisses Baron Friedrich von Hügel, a Roman Catholic mystic and lay theologian) Yeats rejects the high road of Christianity and—by implication—all institutional systems of religious commitment. "Predestined" as an artist to elect "original sin," the matrix of all art, he would instead side once again with "unchristened" Homer; for Samson's riddle ("Out of the strong came forth sweetness"), he suggests, portends resolution of all antinomies. Just as Samson discovered "a swarm of bees and honey" in the carcass of a dead lion, so too would Yeats draw from the fallen natural world the substance of beautiful and truthful art.[38] Living life to the hilt, the swordsman would go "Proud, open-eyed and laughing to the tomb."

In one of his famous meditations Yeats summoned "proud, open-eyed and laughing" John Synge from the tomb to praise him for having recreated the life of a people "passionate and simple like his heart."[39] Synge's great accomplishment of learning to treat death and old age with "objectivity and grim humour"[40] concerns us here because a similar attempt became, from the late 1920s on, one of Yeats's major concerns. Discussing Synge's development, Yeats may as well have been describing his own: "In Synge's early unpublished work . . . there is brooding melancholy and morbid self-pity. He had to undergo an aesthetic transformation, analogous to religious conversion, before he became the audacious, joyous, ironical man we know. The emotional life in so far as it was deliberate had to be transferred . . . from a condition of self-regarding melancholy to its direct opposite. This transformation must have seemed to him a discovery of his true self, of his true moral being."[41] Surely, we may say of Yeats, as he did of Synge, that though "dying," he "chose the living world for text."

François Villon, who supplied Yeats with the important last line of "Tom the Lunatic" ("In that faith I live or die")[42] and who is mentioned frequently in Yeats's prose writings, has been termed influential in the development of Synge's outlook and style. T. R. Henn, who observes that Yeats did not come to treat unpleasant earthiness successfully until the Crazy Jane and Old Tom poems, says that Yeats's new mastery is derived, "in some parts, through Synge from Villon."[43] "Villon," he adds, "seems to have appealed in a special manner to Irish writers."[44] Synge translated several of his poems (Synge's *Poems and Translations* was published in 1909 by Yeats's Cuala Press), and several of Yeats's poet friends of the Nineties (Ernest Dowson, for example), anxious perhaps to identify with this audacious and hounded continental forerunner, expressed great admiration for him.

Villon did appeal especially to Yeats, and he deserves to figure prominently in study of Yeats's old age. In 1906, discussing "why the blind man in ancient times was made a poet," Yeats said: "In primitive times the blind man became a poet, as he became a fiddler in our village, because he had to be driven out of activities all his nature cried for, before he could be contented with the praise of life. And often it is Villon or Verlaine with impediments plain to all, who sings of life with the ancient simplicity."[45] We recall that, though cast in "the frog-spawn of a blind man's ditch," the Self was content to accept its lot as "a blind man battering blind men"; now Yeats, deprived of "all his nature called for," becomes the fiddler of *Words for Music Perhaps*. In 1925, explaining his affinity to Villon, Yeats once again foretold his own development: "It is very likely because I am a poet and not a painter that I feel so much more keenly that suffering of Villon—of the 13th Phase as man, and of it or near it in epoch—in whom the human soul for the first time stands alone before a death ever present to imagination, without help from a Church that is fading away; or is it that I remember Aubrey Beardsley, a man of like phase though of different epoch, and so read into Villon's suffering our modern conscience which gathers intensity as we approach the close of an era? Intensity that has seemed to me pitiless self-judgment may have been but heroic gaiety."[46]

Admiring the folk speech of some passages from Synge, Yeats once noted that they have "the flavour of Homer, of the Bible, of Villon."[47] Thus with these three we return to the question of the "unchristened heart" and of the poet who, "impediments plain to all," refused heavenly mansions in order to sing of life with all "the ancient simplicity."

Certain artists, Yeats observes, "through passion become conjoint to their buried selves."[48] This is precisely what happened to Yeats. Acquiring late in life what he had earlier ascribed to Dante and Villon as the "Vision of Evil," like those poets he came to understand that his "fate wrecked what life could not rebuild." Had he "cherished any species of optimism," unlike them he would have had to remain amidst Byzantine artifice, "a false beauty," and thus would have "suffered no change at all." We must admire Yeats for the same reason that he gazed "in awe" at Dante and Villon: like these men "mirrored in all the suffering of desire," in his final years Yeats came to attain ever greater achievements because he re-created "from terror" not only works of art, but a "new species of man" born "through that art." As Yeats praised these "masters," so too must we praise him: "They and their sort alone earn contemplation, for it is only when the intellect has wrought the whole of life to drama, to crisis, that we may live for contemplation, and yet keep our intensity."

The whole of his life turned to drama, Yeats contemplated and gathered intensity. As he had written of Villon, Yeats too passed from suffering to intensity, and thence to "pitiless self-judgment" and "heroic gaiety," the alternating moods of *Last Poems*. Four days after his seventieth birthday he wrote to his new friend,

Lady Gerald Wellesley: "A ferment has come upon my imagination. If I write more poetry it will be unlike anything I have done."[49] A few months later he wrote: "My public life I will pare down to almost nothing. My imagination is on fire again."[50] The following year, recalling that Ernest Dowson had written of "wine and women and song," "bitter and gay" things, he remarked, "It never occurred to me to wonder why the Dowson I knew seemed neither gay nor bitter"; and noting that his early association with Dowson and others of the Rhymers' Club had been characterized by "crude speculation that made me ashamed," he remembered praying that his imagination "be fixed upon life itself."[51] The "bitter and gay" quality of his later work was made possible only by fixing his imagination on "crisis," on "life itself."

To Ethel Mannin he wrote in 1935, "I want to make a last song, sweet and exultant, a sort of European *geeta*, or rather my *geeta*, not doctrine but song."[52] The "trembling of the veil of the temple," though not as he originally had imagined it, he felt to be imminent again. A year later we read: "I am well—my blood pressure very low & my heart is well. I can now sleep lying flat but I am physically but not mentally weak. At last I shall, I think, sing the heroic song I have longed for—perhaps my swan song."[53]

CHAPTER THREE ✳ UNFASHIONABLE GYRES

I HAVE CONSTRUCTED a myth," Yeats wrote to Olivia Shakespear as he finished a draft of *A Vision*, "but then one can believe in a myth—one only assents to philosophy."[1] Though aspects of this complicated cosmological myth are frequently reflected in Yeats's poetry, the poems themselves are eminently readable without more than a passing acquaintance with details of Yeats's elaborate system of cones, gyres, wheels, and whatnot.

Important for us here, however, is to recognize the form assumed by Yeats's contemplations of time. Brooding upon the whirl of history, he fixed his thoughts into a metaphysic of order central to which is the spiral nature of the temporal continuum. For Yeats, the movement of history is neither rectilinear nor circular; rather, time moves according to the motion of interlocking cones, the "bobbin" of each age unwinding what another has bound. Of this "private philosophy" Yeats said in 1938: "To me all things are made of the conflict of two states of consciousness, beings or persons which die each other's life, live each other's death. That is true of life and death themselves. Two cones (or whirls), the apex of each in the other's base."[2] Hence, his schematization of the historical process, while allowing for "progress,"

34

also establishes a basis for continuity and demands an awareness of tradition. The intricate apparatus mapped out for us in *A Vision* not only constitutes a pattern according to which temporal events and human types occur and recur, but also provides correspondences whereby they may be compared and related. As he wrote in his 1930 diary, "History seems to me a human drama, keeping the classical unities by the clear division of its epochs, turning one way or the other because this man hates or that man loves. . . . Yet the drama has its plot, and this plot ordains character and passions and exists for their sake."[3]

The principal virtue of this myth, important features of which Yeats termed "stylistic arrangements of experience comparable to the cubes in the drawings of Wyndham Lewis and to the ovoids in the sculpture of Brancusi,"[4] is that they provided him with perspective. In a confused age of confusing ideologies, where in order to transcend the discontinuous terms of their existence some turned for synthesis to Marx, others to Freud, and still others (hoping not to turn again) turned to Lancelot Andrewes[5] —Yeats looked to the phases of the moon. His supernatural "instructors," who had promised to give him metaphors for poetry, did so by suggesting an axis of vision whence he could view history as a coherent whole.

Each age unwinds the thread bound by another age, Yeats was fond of saying. Civilizations, like the phases of the moon, wax and wane according to foreordained cycles plotted by the gyres of time: "It amuses me to remember that before Phidias and his westward-moving art, Persia fell, and when full moon came round again, amid eastward-moving thought, and brought Byzantine glory, Rome fell; and that at the outset of our westward-moving Renaissance Byzantium fell; all things dying each other's life, living each other's death."[6]

One of the most awesome of Yeats's works concerned with such mutations of history is *The Resurrection*, which bears brief mention here because it is framed by two important late poems. Set during the juncture of the classical and Christian eras, the play dramatizes the import of the cataclysmic transition that took place when Christianity, a "primary" force surging out of the chaotic East, obliterated with blood and mystery the rational balance and order of "antithetical" Hellenic civilization. As the singers of the closing song proclaim,

> *The Babylonian starlight brought*
> *A fabulous, formless darkness in;*
> *Odour of blood when Christ was slain*
> *Made all Platonic tolerance vain*
> *And vain all Doric discipline.*[7]

Especially in its formidable opening and closing songs, the play juxtaposes opposing cycles of civilization while establishing correspondences between Virgo and Mary, Dionysus and Christ, Spica (the star which Virgo carries in her hand) and the Star of Bethlehem. (It seems appropriately ironic that Yeats should, in the closing lines of the song quoted above, use a cross figure— chiasmus—to underscore the vanity of Hellenic *paideia*.) Christ, neither the simulacrum of the rational Greek who would subtly distinguish between appearance and reality, nor the all too human (therefore misguided) pretender-Messiah of the earthy and pragmatic Hebrew, ushers in a new dispensation, the significance of which terrifies the Greek: "O Athens, Alexandria, Rome, something has come to destroy you. The heart of a phantom is beating. Man has begun to die. Your words are clear at last, O Heraclitus. God and men die each other's life, live each other's death." The Greek persists in defining human knowledge as that which "keeps the road from here to Persia free from robbers, that has built the beautiful humane cities, that has made the modern world, that stands between us and the barbarian"; but the Syrian, shocked into recognition, divines the future more clearly when he asks, "What if there is always something that lies outside knowledge, outside order? What if at the moment when knowledge and order seem complete that something appears?"[8]

In "The Second Coming" Yeats had voiced a similar theme. In this apocalypse crowded with images of inhuman power, Yeats, staring eastward, foresees the brutal and inevitable consequences of "twenty centuries of stony sleep . . . vexed to nightmare by a rocking cradle." Not only destruction of equilibrium and desecration of "innocence," but fearful transvaluation of everything that man esteems would be brought by the blood tide soon to be loosed by a new turn of the gyres. "Surely some revelation is at hand." Momentarily, the prophetic speaker sees into the womb of time: "And what rough beast, its hour come round at last,/ Slouches towards Bethlehem to be born?"

"What if the irrational return? What if the circle begin again?"

the Syrian had asked. A decade later, once again contemplating the revolution of gyres and the "irrational streams of blood" attending the general disorder that they bring round, Yeats cried, "What matter?" Repeated four times in "The Gyres" (the introductory poem of *Last Poems and Plays*) and setting the tone for much to follow, the cry heralds the heroic affirmation toward which his work had been evolving. "Rejoice!" booms a voice from the depths of a cavern, and thus rejoicing Yeats prophesies another resurrection, a restoration of faded glories. Rejoicing in his apprehension of the principle of change itself, he attained the heroic posture of "tragic joy," a mode of existence whereby the knowing man may withstand the tawdriness of today by attuning himself to the inevitable promise of tomorrow. This growing understanding not only of the pattern of historical process but of its existential corollaries as well is largely responsible for that attainment of greater awareness which in 1935 he termed "heroic discipline." He told Dorothy Wellesley: "I think that the true poetic movement of our time is towards some heroic discipline. . . . 'Bitter and gay,' that is the heroic mood. When there is despair, public or private, when settled order seems lost, people look for strength within or without. Auden, Spender, all that seem the new movement *look* for strength in Marxian Socialism, or in Major Douglas; they want marching feet. The lasting expression of our time is not this obvious choice but in a sense of something steel-like and cold within the will, something passionate and cold."[9]

Yeats was convinced that the steadily declining civilized values of modern times were breaking down even more radically. "Europe is in the waning Moon," he said, "are all those things that we love waning?" "The present state of Europe" and his "attempt to find a poetical emotion" with which to dispel the "passions" besetting him, he explained to Dorothy Wellesley in December 1936, were greatly responsible for the mental and physical exhaustion plaguing him. Characteristically enough, however, he added, "my emotional crisis has given me a theme for one of my more considerable poems, in the metre of *Sailing to Byzantium*."[10] "The Gyres," a "passionate and cold" poem, sets forth Yeats's "sense of something steel-like and cold within the will," something that pierces beyond the immediate and contingent and sees into the nature of all things.

In the first stanza, the dramatic speaker, beholding the destruc-
tive movement of the gyres and apostrophizing them as well
("The gyres! The gyres!"), enjoins his alter ego, "Old Rocky
Face," to "look forth," that is, to observe what the gyres are
doing, and—more important—to look to the future. Cosmic up-
heaval, dooming everything we cherish, has forced us to think
in unaccustomed ways. Because "things thought too long can be
no longer thought," we must accommodate ourselves to new
perspectives, those which move us to "laugh in tragic joy."

"Old Rocky Face" has been the subject of much critical conjecture. The image, an especially rich one, is undoubtedly composite, and must be construed that way. Whatever the source, it
seems clear that "Old Rocky Face" represents—as the adjectives
indicate—the enduring aspect of Yeats's being, the antithetical
self responsible for poetic creation. "I think he fashioned from
his opposite," he wrote of Dante, "an image that may have been
a stony face."[11] Critics, with good reason, have associated the
image with the Sphinx (undoubtedly because of its timeless and
inscrutable stare), Blake's Urizen, and the Delphic Oracle.[12]
More direct is a possible allusion to a stone face carved on the
southeast wall of Yeats's tower looking toward the ruins of Coole.

I think, however, that A. Norman Jeffares, who links "Old
Rocky Face" with Shelley's Ahasuerus, comes closest to locating
the probable literary source.[13] In some early drafts Yeats wrote
"Old cavern man,"[14] thus alluding, consciously or otherwise, to
the Jew of *Hellas* who "dwells in a sea-cavern/'Mid the Demon-
esi," and who is so old that

> *He seems to have outlived a world's decay;*
> *The hoary mountains and the wrinkled ocean*
> *Seem younger still than he . . .*
>
> . . .
>
> *. . . But from his eye looks forth*
> *A life of unconsumèd thought which pierces*
> *The Present, and the Past, and the To-come.*[15]

In "The Trembling of the Veil" Yeats wrote of his fascination
with Ahasuerus: "In later years my mind gave itself to gregarious
Shelley's dream of . . . his old man, master of all human knowledge, hidden from human sight in some shell-strewn cavern on
the Mediterranean shore."[16] The "one passage above all" from
Hellas which Yeats said "ran perpetually in my ears," begins:

> *Some feign that he is Enoch: others dream*
> *He was pre-Adamite, and has survived*
> *Cycles of generation and of ruin.*[17]

"Old Rocky Face," like Ahasuerus, sees "the birth of this old world through all its cycles/Of desolation and of loveliness."[18] Further relations with *Hellas* may be established when we consider that both Shelley and Yeats, concerned with historical recurrence and better things to come, echo Virgil's famous *Fourth Eclogue,* interpreted messianically during the Middle Ages.[19] Not only did Virgil prophesy the return of the Golden Age and its heroic deeds, but he also announced: "The Fates have spoken in concord with the unalterable decrees of destiny. 'Run, spindles,' they have said. 'This is the pattern of the age to come.' "[20] Moreover, in *Hellas* and "The Gyres" Shelley and Yeats display a profound concern for the problem of freedom. Just as freedom, in its socio-political formulation, motivated much of Shelley's endeavor, so too its existential and artistic aspects engaged Yeats. Although Yeats shares neither Shelley's doctrine of progress nor his romantic optimism, the concept of "tragic joy" (developed more fully in "Lapis Lazuli") results in great measure from attempting to discover the terms according to which human freedom is possible. Many of Yeats's poems, we shall see, probe this question and illustrate its terms.

These correspondences do much to identify the speaker of the poem with the future. This, of course, is Yeats's intention, the end toward which the poem obviously moves. (Curtis Bradford's manuscript study suggests to him that Yeats first wrote what is now stanza three, and that "the whole poem grew out of the comforting idea with which the finished poem ends. . . ."[21] "Old Rocky Face," a metaphor of permanence, suggests a principle that survives all while all else passes away. Especially when read in the light of "Old cavern man" of early drafts, it recalls not only the "cavern" from which gods are resurrected and cycles reversed, but the "Cavern" which Spengler (whose *Decline of the West* Yeats had read), while discussing "a metaphysic of Last Things," called "the prime symbol of the coming Culture."[22] Additional metaphysical significance accrues to this stone image when, as with the reborn Christ of *The Resurrection* and the awakening Sphinx of "The Second Coming," we think of a "broken sepulchre." Here, however—and the difference is crucial

—the "broken sepulchre" promises disinterment of things of value. Though in "The Gyres" he once again accents universal mutability—"Worlds on worlds are rolling ever/From creation to decay"[23]—the promise of the future is that "all things" will "run/On that unfashionable gyre again."

Fundamentally, Yeats's attitude in "The Gyres" is one of acceptance. In this connection, it would profit us to note how far he has progressed from the moody introspection of his youth. The objective stone and cavern imagery here contrasts sharply with, for example, the subjective "twisted, echo-harbouring shell" of his "The Song of the Happy Shepherd." Though the cavern of the former poem and the convoluted chambers of the latter both echo "comfort" to one distressed by the passing of comfortable worlds, there is a world of difference between the sea-shell's "melodious guile" and the forthright "Rejoice!" heard from the cavern. Though for the fretful shepherd "words alone are certain good," the "passionate and cold" aged poet requires but "one word," the only one, indeed, that the voice in the cavern knows.

Through various forms of dream, we have seen, Yeats's heroes almost invariably have sought escape, never really realizing in their agony that "in dreams begins responsibility." But now, facing the full reality of their depressing circumstances, and understanding its whys and wherefores, Yeats discovers the secret of heroism: "Does not the soldier become the sage . . . when some Elizabethan tragedy makes him reply to a threat of hanging: 'What has that to do with me?' "[24] With this evocation of "What matter?" comes the realization that (we might say) in responsibility begins freedom—"Rejoice!" From the knowledge of—as he must have remembered from *Hellas*—

> *How cities, on which Empire sleeps enthroned,*
> *Bow their towered crests to mutability,*[25]

comes the further realization of the rationale of human freedom itself:

> *Hector is dead and there's a light in Troy;*
> *We that look on but laugh in tragic joy.*

Reference to the death of Hector indicates that another cycle is drawing to a close. Following the conjunction (and thus juxtaposed to the bare statement of Hector's fate), the laconic "there's a light in Troy" does much to suggest the attitude with which, at this crucial time, one achieves "tragic joy." We should note that "light" refers not only to the fire of burning Troy but also to the "illumination" afforded to beholders of that tragic scene. Thus, the onlooker is "fired" with tragic joy in much the same way as are the tragic heroes of "Lapis Lazuli," where, after "Black out," they are illumined and transfigured by the blazing light of "Heaven."

Events of the past, as they relate to the present, expand the context of the poem to include details of an era recently come to an end, the time of the Troubles. The "irrational streams of blood" which stain the earth recall the "dragon-ridden," disordered days of Civil War sketched so compellingly in "Nineteen Hundred and Nineteen." Among the "ancient lineaments"—the noun is striking for its overtones of sharpness and clarity—now "blotted out" are Lady Gregory and landscaped Coole, both of proud and ancient lineage. The intimidations of a "drunken soldiery" could not breach her pride and strength of spirit. Numbering her in his song of "Beautiful Lofty Things," Yeats assigned her to the vanished race of "Olympians": "Yesterday he threatened my life./I told him that nightly from six to seven I sat at this table,/The blinds drawn up." Of Lady Gregory and the generation he outlived—"A greater, a more gracious time has gone"—Yeats had declared a few years earlier in "Coole Park and Ballylee, 1931":

> We were the last romantics—chose for theme
> Traditional sanctity and loveliness;
> Whatever's written in what poets name
> The book of the people; whatever most can bless
> The mind of man or elevate a rhyme;
> But all is changed, that high horse riderless,
> Though mounted in that saddle Homer rode
> Where the swan drifts upon a darkening flood.

Whether of Arnold's dismal plain or of Yeats's lonely flood, the darkness is universal and covers all. These streams of blood, an emblem of ignorance and brutal irrationality, also suggest the "formless" tide of "darkness" that engulfed Greek equilibrium and left "odour of blood" in the passing wake of "Platonic tolerance" and "Doric discipline."

Echoes of earlier thought and previous works also enrich the fifth and sixth lines of stanza two: "For painted forms or boxes

of make-up/In ancient tombs I sighed, but not again." Though
graciously resisting conversion to Christianity ("So get you gone,
Von Hügel, though with blessings on your head"), Yeats had
noted in "Vacillation" that "The body of Saint Teresa lies undecayed in tomb,/Bathed in miraculous oil, sweet odours from
it come." We remember that he spurned "what seems most wel-
come in the tomb" in order to play his "predestined" role:
"Homer is my example and his unchristened heart." He told
Mrs. Shakespear: "I feel that this is the choice of the saint (St.
Theresa's ecstasy, Gandhi's smiling face): comedy; and the heroic
choice: Tragedy (Dante, Don Quixote). Live Tragically but be
not deceived (not the fool's Tragedy). Yet I accept all the miracles. Why should not the old embalmers come back as ghosts
and bestow upon the saint all the care once bestowed upon
Rameses? Why should I doubt the tale that when St. Theresa's
tomb was opened in the middle of the nineteenth century, the
still undecayed body dripped with fragrant oil?"[26] Much given
to antinomies, even in his treatment of the "miraculous" Yeats
displays purposeful ambiguity of vision. In *The Winding Stair*
we also find "Oil and Blood," where "tombs of gold and lapis
lazuli" house the still fragrant embalmed bodies of holy men and
women; "But under heavy loads of trampled clay" lie vampire
bodies "full of blood," bloody and wet like their frightful shrouds
and lips. Observing that these "at once similar and dissimilar"
images "are given the semblance of logical connection by 'But,'
the opening word of the second stanza," William York Tindall
writes: "Not logic, however, but creative contiguity explains the
feeling of the poem. As for idea: the two visions produce a composite vision, larger than either, that carries an undefinable commentary upon man's life and times."[27]

   In its associative richness, then, the second stanza of "The
Gyres" reveals a situation characteristic of metaphysical and
symbolist poetry: the coexistence and concomitance of logically
disjunctive elements. Here, the correlative and complementary
conditions of terror and ecstasy prepare us for the "Rejoice!"
which closes the stanza; at the same time, the terror-ecstasy paradox follows from its analogue, "tragic joy," at the end of the
previous stanza. Indeed, much of the form and feeling of these
two stanzas—and the "composite vision" of the poem as a whole
—results from a rationale of "creative contiguity."

Men as well as gyres and poems run their course "between extremities." When "a brand, or flaming breath" comes to banish "All those antinomies/Of day and night," Yeats says in the opening section of "Vacillation," the body deems it "death" and the heart "remorse." If "these be right," he puzzles, "What is joy?" To face reality squarely, Yeats discovered, he must approach as Homer, perhaps "many-minded Homer," "mad as the mist and snow." Confronted by antinomies and bewildered by "joy," he must nevertheless reject not only the "melodious guile" of Von Hügel's comforting words and their promise of perfection, but all other forms of "artifice" as well. In "The Gyres" he sees such artifice and "miracle" ("painted forms or boxes of make-up/In ancient tombs") to be as vain as the miraculous golden bird of "Sailing to Byzantium." For these "I sighed, but not again."

The tomb which does concern him now he presents as an image of renewal:

> *Those that Rocky Face holds dear,*
> *Lovers of horses and of women, shall,*
> *From marble of a broken sepulchre,*
> *Or dark betwixt the polecat and the owl,*
> *Or any rich, dark nothing disinter*
> *The workman, noble and saint, and all things run*
> *On that unfashionable gyre again.*

With a new turn of the gyres this tomb will break asunder and the purified earth will witness the re-emergence of "workman, noble and saint," the hardy trinity of Yeats's commonwealth.

The related "dark betwixt the polecat and the owl" and "any rich, dark nothing" from which these worthies may emerge presents something of a puzzle. Why does Yeats locate thus the source of the coming culture? "From marble of a broken sepulchre," with its manifold associations of endurance and renewal, seems clear enough, but what of what follows? Rightly doubting "whether it is possible to fix the meaning entirely," T. R. Henn nevertheless seems content to observe only that the polecat may be associated with destruction, the owl with wisdom and the supernatural, and both with desolate places and ruins. He ends his brief discussion of these lines by noting merely that "betwixt" is ambiguous.[28] In her explication of "The Gyres," Vivienne Koch fails to come to terms with the image. Her statement, "It is typical of Yeats's method that he saw no contradiction between the 'irrational streams of blood' as defiling earth and man, and the same instinctual sources ('rich, dark nothing') as generating the new cycle of fulfilment," not only begs the question but confuses it as well by needlessly attributing contradiction to Yeats's reasoning.[29]

The polecat and the owl, I would urge, represent the two elements of a reciprocal relationship; together they suggest the ordering of opposites into a state of dynamic equilibrium. The image suggests this state because, though both animals are creatures of prey, the former is a mammal that hunts fowl, while the latter is a fowl that hunts mammals; whereas the one looks "up" for its prey, the other looks "down."[30] Indeed, to schematize this relationship would be to sketch the relationship of the interlocking gyres of *A Vision*.

"Dark," defining the common bound of two interlocking gyres, suggests not only the "place" where one era rises as the other falls, but also—especially with the addition of the second form of the image[31]—the lonely locale of "antithetical" beings out of place in our "primary" times:[32] the cavern of Old Rocky Face, the wilderness of clamoring prophets and contemplative saints, the fecund inner world of aristocrats, artists, and artisans. Awaiting the hour of their disinterment, they now bide their time in the matrix of their "proper dark."[33]

The pattern implicit in the central image of this stanza provides us, then, with an analogue for the relationship of Concord and Discord, the Empedoclean principles alluded to in the first stanza which Yeats used in *A Vision* to illustrate interlocking gyres, "the fundamental symbol of my instructors."[34] Though "Empedocles has thrown all things about;/Hector is dead and there's a light in Troy," onlookers can "laugh in tragic joy" if they are able to detect beyond chaos and corruption such immutable patterns of order as Yeats metaphorically reveals in the final stanza.

Nearly seven lines of the final stanza comprise but a single sentence. Though its suspended cadences roll impressively to heightened climax, the stanza nevertheless does end on a discordant note: *run::again*. This dissonance in the closing couplet is an analogue, I would think, for the questioning taking place in Yeats's mind as he bids "Old Rocky Face" to "look forth." Yet the fact remains that "History"—as Yeats himself declared—"is necessity until it takes fire in someone's head and becomes freedom or virtue."[35] As time and history took fire in his imagination, he came to discover the exhilarating joy of life sparked by the smart of tragic circumstance. And with this discovery came increased understanding of the perplexing and often painful conditions that may illuminate human existence and make it more meaningful. "The last knowledge has often come most quickly to turbulent men, and for a season brought new turbulence," he once wrote of Dante.[36] Though Auden's elegy laconically reminds us that "poetry makes nothing happen," it remains for us to seek further insights into the nature of that knowledge and turbulence.

CHAPTER FOUR ✱ TRAGIC GAIETY

As many of his last poems remind us, this "new turbulence" was for Yeats an "hour of terror" that "comes to test the soul."[1] To a radio audience in 1936 he announced: "I think profound philosophy must come from terror. An abyss opens under our feet; inherited convictions, the pre-suppositions of our thoughts, those Fathers of the Church Lionel Johnson expounded, drop into the abyss."[2] Yeats was speaking from experience. Illness during the late winter and spring of 1936 (this time severe breathlessness indicative of the dropsical condition that was to cause his death) took him to Majorca, where with his "unchristened heart" he once again plumbed tomblike depths of terror. Peering into the abyss, Yeats suffered recurrent dreams of death and embodied these frightening experiences in "The Apparitions." Thrice intoning an awesome refrain, *"Fifteen apparitions have I seen;/The worst a coat upon a coat-hanger,"* the speaker recoils from "the increasing Night" now come to confront him.[3] Familiar enough is the echo of "a tattered coat upon a stick" of "Sailing to Byzantium," but unusual for the poetry of Yeats's maturity is the use of a capitalized abstraction, especially in a key position. Tomblike, it is "Night" that threatens annihilation of the speaker's mortal person. Now, Yeats's problem is not so much adjusting to old age as it is accepting it, and accepting it while shoring up within himself "all that strength" capable of endowing the heart with ever-deepening joy. Time has brought a new antinomy, one between achievement and oblivion.

"Lapis Lazuli," perhaps the most accomplished poem of this period, is inspired by and grounded in this antinomy of achievement and oblivion, ecstasy and terror.[4] Here, summoning strength to resist and transcend the "mystery and fright" of ubiquitous darkness, Yeats finally resolves "all those antinomies/Of day and night," and in so doing answers "What is joy?", the overwhelming question to which they lead. If achievement in creation, self-realization, brings joy that "grows more deep day after day," the oblivion of "increasing Night" introduces the makings of high tragedy. Synthesizing from these components, Yeats achieves resolution by way of paradox: "tragic joy." Thus, from the abyss, from terror, comes "profound philosophy," "that tragic ecstasy which is the best that art—perhaps that life—can give."[5] As though looking ahead, he had written in 1917: "I shall find the dark glow luminous, the void fruitful when I understand I have nothing, that the ringers in the tower have appointed for the hymen of the soul a passing bell."[6]

A year before composing "Lapis Lazuli" Yeats wrote to Dorothy Wellesley: "I notice that you have much lapis lazuli; someone has sent me a present of a great piece carved by some Chinese sculptor into the semblance of a mountain with temple, trees, paths and an ascetic and pupil about to climb the mountain. Ascetic, pupil, hard stone, eternal theme of the sensual east. The heroic cry in the midst of despair. But no, I am wrong, the east has its solutions always and therefore knows nothing of tragedy. It is we, not the east, that must raise the heroic cry."[7] As we have seen, "The Gyres" is one such heroic cry. As for "Lapis Lazuli," the cry, transfiguring "dread" to "gaiety," moves on several levels of implication. Tragic joy, what comes when man "completes his partial mind,"[8] brings about the utmost degree of fulfillment both for man and for the fallen world forming the matrix of his art. This is so because tragic joy is creative: not only does it integrate personality—tighten the bolts of one's being, so to speak—but, manifesting itself in the aesthetic urge, integrates in its shaping vision the chaotic world without. (The "mystery of esthetic," as Joyce's Stephen put it, is the mystery of a transfigurative act.) In the midst of despair, under the press

of tragic events, Yeats says, great men become "gay"; like great
art, they are shaped to wholeness, harmony, and radiance. Moreover, as metaphysical insight discovers a persevering *logos* in the
whirl of flux, so too the tragic hero. "We sing amid our uncertainty," Yeats once wrote.[9] His eyes "twinkling" and "gay,"
heroic man sings for every tatter of mortality, and in singing
affirms and exercises his will to create and re-create even when
all creation seems doomed. As gay Seanchan proclaims in *The
King's Threshold* to the youngest of his scholars:

> *And I would have all know that when all falls*
> *In ruin, poetry calls out in joy,*
> *Being the scattering hand, the bursting pod,*
> *The victim's joy among the holy flame,*
> *God's laughter at the shattering of the world.*[11]

The language and rhythm of the first stanza of "Lapis Lazuli,"
those of common speech, at once describe and judge those who
would spurn art because of the mechanical terror threatened by
"Aeroplane and Zeppelin." To a world caught in compounding
crisis, the "bomb-balls" likely to be pitched by "King Billy" are
cause enough for "hysterical" activists to set aside the claims of
gaiety-inspiring art. Rambling and nonchalant, the first section's
flat cadences of simple statement heavily underscored by easy
alliteration not only tacitly condemn the easy defeatism of weak
"women," but provide ample contrast to the tragic stance majes-
tically measured in the succeeding section. That "hysterical
women," a metaphor for anti-heroic behavior, expresses contempt
for all frenzied sissies is all the more plain when we consider that
hysteria is derived from Greek *hystera*, womb. Homely "King
Billy" alludes to William of Orange, whose army at the Battle of
the Boyne in 1690 defeated James II and thus doomed the Irish
Catholic cause as well as Stuart hopes of restoration.[10] At the
same time, "King Billy" recalls Kaiser Wilhelm II and the Zeppelin raids on London.[11] The first four lines rhyme perfectly,
but the last four, ending on great dissonances (*done:in, out:flat*),
suggest by their irresolution the imperfect attitude of "hysterical
women" and the inadequacy of their philosophy of "action."

The second section, in contrast, is written in the grand manner
characteristic of many poems of *The Tower* and *The Winding
Stair*. Theatrical imagery, stemming from the Shakespearean
notion that all the world's a stage and men the players thereon,

governs the entire section. By its very nature drama entails and embodies crisis; and because of its patterned structure it not only allows for the development of crisis, but also demands its shaped containment. A shaped medium, drama becomes a shaping agent as well, both for actors playing roles and for audiences responding cathartically. Though crisis may ultimately lead to a tragic resolution, in doing so it may also command commitments that the free man must not evade if he would live heroically, truly worthy of his freedom. Thus it is that Ophelia, Cordelia, Hamlet, Lear, and all their kind, as existential persons, pursue to the bitter end the commitments upon which their identity is predicated, and in so doing remain true not only to themselves but to the option of heroic resistance to absurdity and annihilation. Art and activism of this higher order are not mutually exclusive, the section shows. If worthy of "their prominent part in the play," truly tragic figures shun hysteria for the heroism of engagement, never breaking up their lines to weep:

> They know that Hamlet and Lear are gay;
> Gaiety transfiguring all that dread.
> All men have aimed at, found and lost;
> Black out; Heaven blazing into the head:
> Tragedy wrought to its uttermost.
> Though Hamlet rambles and Lear rages,
> And all the drop-scenes drop at once
> Upon a hundred thousand stages,
> It cannot grow by an inch or an ounce.

"Shakespeare's persons," Yeats early observed, "when the last darkness has gathered about them, speak out of an ecstasy that is one half the self-surrender of sorrow, and one half the last playing and mockery of the victorious sword before the defeated world."[12] Thirty years later he observed that Shakespearean heroes communicate "through their looks, or through the metaphorical patterns of their speech, the sudden enlargement of their vision, their ecstasy at the approach of death. . . ."[13]

Unlike the incomplete "hysterical women," these tragic figures, "If worthy their prominent part in the play,/Do not break up their lines to weep." The former line is especially heavily charged. We construe: (a) If as actors they deserve the prominent role in which they have been cast; (b) If as men they are worthy of the destiny set before them; (c) If Hamlet (Lear, Ophelia, Cor-

delia) is really the Hamlet (Lear, Ophelia, Cordelia) that Shakespeare's tragic vision envisaged. As for the latter line, Frank
O'Connor relates: "After interfering in a rehearsal to stop a
young actress sobbing at the close of Lady Gregory's 'Dervor-
gilla,' I asked him, 'Is it ever, under any circumstances, permissible
for an actor to weep on the stage?' 'Never,' he said, and turned
it into a poem."[14]

"How strange is the subconscious gaiety that leaps up before
danger or difficulty," Yeats wrote during his 1927 illness.[15] This
is not so strange after all, we now discover, for knowing actors
know that "Hamlet and Lear are gay," that gaiety transfigures
dread, that weeping eyes cannot twinkle. Here, the Lear image
takes us back to the "hysterical women." Two weeks after com-
pleting the poem Yeats told Dorothy Wellesley: "I have never
'produced' a play in verse without showing the actors that the
passion of the verse comes from the fact the speakers are holding
down violence or madness—'down Hysterica passio.' All depends
on the completeness of the holding down. . . ."[16] We recall that,
choked with passion, Lear cries, "Hysterica passio! Down, thou
climbing sorrow,/Thy element's below!"[17]

"It is by the perception of a change, like the sudden 'blacking
out' of the lights of the stage, that passion creates its most violent
sensation," Yeats wrote in "The Trembling of the Veil."[18]
Now, as darkness drops again, the hero experiences the ultimate
paradox of tragedy: simultaneous apprehension of "Black out"
and "Heaven blazing into the head." Tragic destiny, Yeats suggests in this balanced line, does not entail oblivion, non-existence;
rather, by accepting all that life had to offer, heaven-illumined
Hamlet and Lear gained life itself, were "saved." Truly, tragedy
"wrought" them to their "uttermost."

So too Yeats's verse. No longer chanting of luxuriant despair,
of weary "wharves of sorrow" beside a wandering "dim grey sea"
athwart whose tide "we and the labouring world" are wearily
"passing by," Yeats now proclaims that "passive suffering is not
a theme for poetry": "In all the great tragedies, tragedy is a
joy to the man who dies; in Greece the tragic chorus danced.
When man has withdrawn into the quicksilver at the back of
the mirror no great event becomes luminous in his mind."[19]

The impermanence of all civilizations and their magnificent
monuments provides the theme of the next section, where by

juxtaposing conquerors on the march to the sculptor's conquest of motion, Yeats sketches the common fate of all fabulous artifice. All civilizations and the fabled works on which they splendidly "stood for a day" are subject to the leveling law of time. Like drumbeats, the accents of the second line not only punctuate the procession of passing conquerors, but signal as well a dominant idea implicit throughout the stanza: the regularity of rise and fall, restoration and ruin. Though the fate of everything we prize is that of Callimachus' ingenious art, somewhere in the dawn of civilization man discovered an abiding principle that Yeats now proclaims simply and eloquently in the concluding lines:

> All things fall and are built again,
> And those that build them again are gay.

Three ancient figures from the ancient East, presided over by a "long-legged bird," a hovering "symbol of longevity," dominate the fourth section.[20] Carved in the stone, these Chinamen, who like their hermit brother Ribh read the book of life with eyes "made aquiline" by time and tragedy, are prefigured by others of their ancient, patient race: "I have a Chinese painting of three old sages sitting together, one with a deer at his side, one with scroll open at the symbol of yen and yin, those two forms that whirl perpetually, creating and recreating all things."[21]

The last section (a sonnet in itself), focusing on and interpreting the artifact that inspired the poem, unites on many levels numerous earlier motifs. The carved piece of lapis lazuli, its description deliberately made ambiguous, functions here as a symbol of art, and at the same time evokes and exemplifies the tragic scene on which the sages stare. The stone, like the world we live in, shows the scars of time and is therefore imperfect. Yet such imperfection is precisely what the artist must joyfully seize and work upon. Like Shakespeare and Callimachus, the artist must shape into order the disordered world around him, must impose the significant perfection of form on what is essentially formless—something that the "hysterical women" do not understand. In this way, the Chinamen's eyes (detecting order and design), though set "mid many wrinkles," are perpetually "gay." The melody these Chinamen hear may actually be a cheerful one, a song built from sad themes but transfigured by the "accomplished fingers" of the player, who, changed utterly by what his "stare" reveals, has permanently transcended sadness and "dread." If a "mournful" melody is really played, the Chinamen must smile nevertheless because their eyes, carved in shining rock, cannot change their fixed expression ("stare").

On another level, we may say that Yeats actually celebrates the stone's imperfection.[22] It gives him occasion (as John Unterecker has explained) to speculate about the Chinamen's destination, to abandon the carving "for a world constructed in pure imagination."[23] Yet, as we recall the artificial golden bird of the Byzantine emperor, we should note that the carved stone (at once a work of art and an analogue for a work of art) is very much of the here and now, that (unlike the golden bird) it realistically reflects the tragic world to which it belongs. Perhaps this is why the figures carved thereon, as they meditate upon this world with gay and glittering eyes, have earned their immortality. Whereas the old man sailing the seas to Byzantium dreamed of deliverance from "the crime of death and birth,"[24] the ancient Chinamen, contemplating greater mutations, grow wise in the knowledge that "All things fall and are built again,/And those that build them again are gay."

Preparing to die, the aged Yeats declared (in the unpublished final stanza of "The Circus Animals' Desertion," another poem about an artist's involvement with art) that "Even at the approach of the un-imaged night/Man has the refuge of his gaity [sic]."[25] God-given because it is found in the rich darkness of fecund nothingness ("Where there is nothing—there is God!"), gaiety reflects the gift of a type of grace, albeit secular, whereby receptive man is moved to strenuous and ennobling acts of creation. Like Blake's "Ancient of Days," calipers in hand at the act of Creation, Yeats's gaiety-filled artists imbue with the significance of form an infinity of chaos which, awaiting the redemptive touch of creators, must otherwise remain unmeasured and therefore unmighty. In our fallen world, unchanged since Homer made mighty music from the discords of original sin, tragic gaiety inspires knowing artists to raid the low, inarticulate stuff of life in order to create the shaped splendors of heightened art. Knowing the secret of Samson's riddle, their eyes may glitter as they go forth to make honey in the rotting carcasses of the dumb lions of the world.

A gift of grace, tragic gaiety is also our hope of glory, we may learn from "Lapis Lazuli." Its attainment, manifest in height-

ened consciousness, is available to East and West alike, but Western wisdom apprehends it uniquely. Both the Western speaker
of the poem and the contemplative Chinamen discover in the
patterned movement of gyres ("forms that whirl perpetually,
creating and re-creating all things") a universal pattern, but their
responses to this pattern may differ. The ancient Chinamen, like
the "great lord of Chou" in "Vacillation," may perhaps be "cast-
ing off the mountain snow" to announce "the meaning of all
song"—"Let all things pass away." Yeats's speaker, however,
drawing upon another inheritance and thus satisfying another
need, rises not to passive contemplation but to a dynamic of
artistic, heroic action. "The east has its solutions always and
therefore knows nothing of tragedy. It is we, not the east, that
must raise the heroic cry."

Tragic heroism, the legacy and the proper norm of the West,
Yeats insists, is a mode of engagement. This artful life is a means
whereby mortal men may be brought to the fullness of their
being. Rejecting the activism of a hysteria that excludes even the
possibility of such beatitude, tragic heroes affirm the worth and
heed the claims of a radically different form of consciousness.
They must play their prominent parts artistically, for in artistic
enterprise, Yeats seems to be saying, lies our great hope of sur-
mounting the numbness brought by the absurdity of the human
condition. Artistic enterprise enlarges the vision of men who
would otherwise be condemned to see but darkly, and seeing
darkly, to respond hysterically to the challenge of adventurous
living. Like religion, the suggestion follows, artistic conscience
is binding, not only in the ethical sense of presenting imperatives,
but also in the existential sense of "tying back," "tying together"
(re + ligio). And as with conventional religion, so too with the
unifying conventions of art: artistic conscience permits men to
be worked utterly, to suffer actively, and perhaps to die, but also
to be wrought to moral splendor. Again, "when all falls/In ruin,
poetry calls out in joy," because with the descent of terror comes
the possibility of rise, of rebirth from terror to the ecstasy of
the tragic moment.

Near the end of his life Yeats came to fathom what his ancient
Chinamen must have learned much earlier: the paradoxical implications of *crisis*. The Chinese express this concept with two
symbols. One means danger, but the underlying one means opportunity.

CHAPTER FIVE ✳ THE PLAIN OF LIR

THAT THE WAY of the fool is also the way of the wise is one of the remarkable paradoxes of literature. Shakespeare and Cervantes, to name but two of its masters, teach us that life has a habit of cleansing the vision of tragic sinners more sinned against than sinning. What holds true for Lear and Quixote holds as well for Yeats, an equally "foolish, passionate man" who in old age sought for other ways and other masks.

After "Black out," we have seen, comes the blazing reality of "Heaven." "There," indeed—as in the heaven-describing circle poem of that name—is the place for all reconciliations. "I saw in a broken vision," says a character from an early play, "but now all is clear to me. Where there is nothing, where there is nothing—there is God!"—and another, mindful at last, declares:

> *I can explain all now.*
> *Only when all our hold on life is troubled,*
> *Only in spiritual terror can the Truth*
> *Come through the broken mind. . . .*[1]

When, in old age, with the mask of Lear Yeats contemplated the strange reality of "ripeness," the words of such wise men became his own. Like his enlightened Chinamen, men who, too, endure their going hence even as their coming hither, he learned

54

that though everything "drop at once/Upon a hundred thousand stages" and we come to nothing, "intensity is all."[2]

To the end Yeats stood in the thick of everything. Staring at tragic scenes both public and private, he strove to focus his whole being upon truly final things. Though his later life continued to be sweetened by the "manifold illusion" that civilizes and sustains, "savage indignation," piercing mind and breast, persisted in marking his stormy career. Remaking always both poem and poet, Yeats moved further to grandly envisioned but ultimately unresolved ends, to the always "bitter and gay" concurrence of antithetical drives that saw him hurrah "the flowers of Spring" from the battered ramparts of a beleaguered "old black tower" near a cave whose echo cries "Lie down and die." Yet for all that, he kept the faith of the "impure ditch" as, "much falling," he summoned final masks for the continuing assault on ultimate "Truth":

> *Grant me an old man's frenzy,*
> *Myself I must remake*
> *Till I am Timon and Lear*
> *Or that William Blake*
> *Who will beat upon the wall*
> *Till Truth obeyed his call.*

Rising from frank meditation to inspired prayer, the patterns of "An Acre of Grass" are familiar. Not abnegating life, but rising to its complexities, even though he craves "An old man's eagle mind," Yeats here does not take flight on the wings of some golden bird. Rather, like Ribh, with eyes "made aquiline" by "solitary prayer,"[3] he would shape divided worlds into "profane perfection." Equally familiar are the now classic juxtapositions of contraries, which not only serve to define the speaker's present condition, but which give special urgency to his aspirations as well. We note, for example, how active Blake, violently scorning Satanic mills of the mind, is counterpointed to a stirring mouse left to haunt a decaying house. Tyndall, Mill, Darwin, and Huxley, symbolic enemies of his youth, like Shaw turned sewing machine,[4] loom here as ponderous engines of rational intellect which, grinding mere immensities of "rag and bone," preclude penetration to transcendent "Truth."

Weighted by disquieting images of unproductive materiality, the first two stanzas of "An Acre of Grass" reveal the physical degradation of old age and its concomitant conditions of mental disjointedness and artistic sterility. Imagination, the creative faculty, is "loose" because it lacks focus, a vital center from which to assert the claims of life and thus overpower infirmity, incapacity, and limitation. In the succeeding stanzas, Timon, Lear, Blake, and Michelangelo, passionate men all, serve as models for inspired ascent. Makers and movers of worlds, these men display commendable intensity as they bravely seek to stretch the confining perimeter of possible experience.

His hold on life troubled, Yeats sought truth in self-examination. "I am not content," he insists in a late poem ("Are You Content?"); and in "What Then?", though aware of perfected accomplishment, he painfully continues to search beyond. Though "boyish plan" seem perfected, old age is not for satisfaction because ageless creative "work," forever hovering ghostlike, is never really "done." Thus, already suspended between satisfaction and desire, Yeats is further disconcerted by the unmistakable overtones of another insidious question; for implicit in the insistent refrain of Plato's mocking ghost—"What then?" —is the frightful echo of "To what avail?"

What now? This is the question taken up by "broken" Yeats in "The Circus Animals' Desertion" as he informs us of his inability to fasten on new themes for new creation. To explore the fundamental entanglement of life and art, Yeats, once again reviewing his career, focuses on the source of his creative energy and on the direction taken by this energy once poetic effort has been set into motion. He recalls how his personal needs and desires engendered the memorable themes of his earlier years. Private involvements, he admits, moved him to create aesthetic constructs which, once imagined and constructed, dominated his attention. The formal requirements and properties of these aesthetic objects "enchanted" him, he confesses—"Players and painted stage took all my love,/And not those things that they were emblems of."

The final section, modulating to conclusion, leads back to primal causes and Yeats's principal concern. "Those masterful images" brought to perfection because their creator "swerved in naught"—"out of what began?" Though nurtured to completeness in "pure mind," what of their matrix? The question is portentous, the more so when we recall the occasion for the poem. Earlier, in "Among School Children" and "A Dialogue of Self and Soul," unable and unwilling to distinguish "dancer" from "dance," and celebrating "impure" ditches because out of their fecundity all life is engendered, Yeats envisioned blessedness. As once with his mysterious "great-rooted blossomer," so now with these further "heart mysteries." Providing us with pattern as well as resolution, the "heart's progress through the poem (the word *heart* itself strategically placed in each section) becomes, of course, the poem."[5] As in his crucial "Dialogue of Self and Soul," here too Yeats suggests that whatever meaning life may offer emerges only from the rich confusion of the concretions of time.

"Those images that yet/Fresh images beget" led Yeats to the torment of further questioning and self-examination. In "The Man and the Echo," a dialectical poem offering further evidence of heart's disquiet begotten by the begetting of "masterful images," Yeats, stunned by the possibility that some of his literary work may have produced unexpected public consequences, turns his speculations to thoughts of death. "All seems evil until I/ Sleepless would lie down and die," he says, to which the Echo answers "Lie down and die."

Refusing, Yeats argues in the next section that unfinished "work" precludes "judgment," that purgation and "release" come only with the integration of all the objects of thought. In this connection, a statement made to Ethel Mannin very shortly after the poem's composition is revealing: "According to Rilke a man's death is born with him and if his life is successful and he escapes mere "mass death" his nature is completed by its final union with it. In my own philosophy the sensuous image is changed from time to time at predestined moments called *Initiatory Moments*. . . . One sensuous image leads to another because they are never analyzed. At *The Critical Moment* they are dissolved by analysis and we enter by free will pure unified experience. When all the sensuous images are dissolved we meet true death."[6] "Sensuous images," though they constitute the very stuff of art and, indeed, plot the pattern of an artist's career, nevertheless do not promote the "great work" (*work* is used three times in the second section) that will bring his nature to the perfection of its intended "final union."

The alternatives facing him, Yeats had written six or seven years earlier in "The Choice," were "perfection of the life, or of the work." Left now with "the night's remorse," which he then foresaw as a possible consequence of his choice, he is teased by Echo's rejoinder into further thoughts of death. Thus another question to the dark oracle:

> *O Rocky Voice,*
> *Shall we in that great night rejoice?*
> *What do we know but that we face*
> *One another in this place?*

We are faced here with a familiar crisis, but for some time now the terms of resolution have been consistent. Although we may be fascinated by the redemptive and fulfilling aspect of death, "breathless mouths" do not summon when we recognize that all our knowledge is grounded in the world of "dying generations" where, as for "that William Blake," "everything that lives is holy":

> *But hush, for I have lost the theme,*
> *Its joy or night seem but a dream;*
> *Up there some hawk or owl has struck,*
> *Dropping out of sky or rock,*
> *A stricken rabbit is crying out,*
> *And its cry distracts my thought.*[7]

"Here on this lowly ground," Yeats (like Donne) questions but does not repent the conditions of mortality. Though he sees darkly, charity compels him to heed the mundane but binding commitments of the only life he has ever known. The distracting cry of the "stricken rabbit" moves his meditation away from the annihilating grave to the claims of life—all life, all that is begotten, born, and some day must die. Faced suddenly by suffering and a model of mortality, the speaker acknowledges the preciousness of life. As with the spell-breaking lance and stricken starling of *The Wanderings of Oisin*, talismans of the time-bound world, the rabbit here occasions the speaker's return to the painful commitments he would have left behind.

Images of massive rock and broken stone recall "The Gyres," the more so when we recall the great command issuing forth from its oracular cavern: "Rejoice!" Likewise in "The Man and the Echo," for "Shall we in the great night rejoice?" admits of one answer only—"Rejoice!" Both common sense and the echo pattern of the previous two sections make this "answer" inevitable. Further, the concluding lines of the poem may be regarded as a form of echo-answer to the question immediately preceding,

"What do we know but that we face/One another in this place."
The speaker's distraction back to life by the cry of the "stricken
rabbit" is thus paralleled and reinforced by the implied echo of,
hence insistence on, "this place," i.e., earth. Whatever their subject, many of Yeats's last poems are charged with the power of
this compelling theme. Because Yeats's imagination is now finally
"fixed upon life itself," one may indeed say of him as he said of
Villon, "Intensity that has seemed . . . pitiless self-judgment may
have been but heroic gaiety."

In many of these late poems, as with numerous others from the
early works on, heroic gaiety or something akin to it is expressed
in the intensity of dance. Looking back to "The Double Vision
of Michael Robartes," for example, we see a girl dancing in a
circle between figures of Sphinx and Buddha atop "the grey rock
of Cashel." "Mind moved yet seemed to stop/As 'twere a spinning
top," Yeats says of this gyrating emblem of perfection who,
resolving antitheses of inward and outward gaze represented by
the two figures, breezily "outdanced thought." Always symbolic
of ordered creativity and the ritual patterns of art and "mystery,"
whirling dancers of this sort fascinated Yeats and other late romantics. Arthur Symons' admiration is typical: "Nothing is stated,
there is no intrusion of words used for the irrelevant purpose of
describing . . . and the dancer, with her gesture, all pure symbol,
evokes from her mere beautiful motion, idea, sensation, all that
one need ever know of event."[8] "It is the dancer's movement,"
Frank Kermode observes, "and the fact that this movement is
passionate, controlled not by intellect but by rhythm and the
demands of plastic form, that make her an emblem of joy
(Symons uses the word) and give her a fantastic reality. . . ."[9]

Celebrations of fantastic realities, poems such as "Imitated from
the Japanese," "Sweet Dancer," "A Crazed Girl," and "A
Drunken Man's Praise of Sobriety" employ dance imagery to
express joyful, intense states of being. The ecstatic speaker of the
first poem (made from a *hokku*), associating the arrival of spring
with the fulfillment of his old age, is moved to dance by his
recognition of this "astonishing" double flowering. Margot Ruddock,[10] imaged simultaneously in a pair of poems as "sweet
dancer" and "crazed girl," finds wholeness in the whirl of the
inspired dance that leads her from her crowd of youthful con-
fusions to the solitary and unifying triumph of ripe art. Whether

gyring on "leaf-sown" garden grass or cluttered seashore, she too, "heroically lost, heroically found," must be numbered in Yeats's catalogue of "beautiful lofty things." Her "desperate music" intoxicates because through its mystery are revealed at once the inspiration, condition, and effect of all artistic transformation.

Drink, dance, and declaration bring this group of poems to a staggering end. "A Drunken Man's Praise of Sobriety" finds the speaker himself now "wound, wound, wound" in circular swishings of a most uncommon sort. Sobriety and drunkenness, life and death—all mere distinctions—go by the boards. Whether high or higher, parody or vision, the effort engages.[11] Syllogizing furiously, Yeats forsakes logic for the headier resolution of happy chiasmus: "A drunkard is a dead man,/And all dead men are drunk." Let these terrible beauties dance on, Yeats insists throughout these poems, for they "fling into my meat/A crazy juice that makes the pulses beat."[12]

" 'Bitter and gay,' that is the heroic mood," Yeats reflected in 1935.[13] A year later, at the same time that he was apostrophizing gay dancers, he threw himself wholeheartedly into bitter public controversy. "I am in a rage," he wrote Ethel Mannin on 15 November 1936. "I have just got a book published by the Talbot Press called *The Forged Casement Diaries*. It is by a Dr. Maloney I knew in New York and he has spent years collecting evidence. He has proved that the diaries, supposed to prove Casement 'a Degenerate' and successfully used to prevent an agitation for his reprieve, were forged. Casement was not a very able man but he was gallant and unselfish, and had surely his right to leave what he would have considered an unsullied name."[14] "Casement forgeries (rage that men of honour should do such things)," he told Dorothy Wellesley a month and a half later, were among those "passions" that had made him ill from "mental strain" and had kept him abed.[15]

"Roger Casement" is one of two inspired but undistinguished ballads written in his "Attempt to find a poetical emotion/To disolve [sic] those passions."[16] "A ferocious ballad written to a popular tune," Yeats said of it. "I heard my ballad sung last night. It is a stirring thing."[17] "Meeting W. B. Y. just after his 'Roger Casement,' Joseph Hone adds, "I was astonished by the ferocity of his feelings. He almost collapsed after reading the verses and had to call for a little port wine." [18]

The ballad was first published on 2 February 1937 in De Valera's *Irish Press*, not the *Irish Times*, where Yeats had first submitted it,[19] on which occasion he told Dorothy Wellesley (28 November 1936) that it "denounces by name _____ and _____ for their share in abetting the forgeries. I shall not be happy until I hear that it is sung by Irish undergraduates at Oxford."[20]

The *Irish Press* version, singling out Alfred Noyes for his part in defaming Casement ("Come Alfred Noyes and all the troup"), drew a disclaimer from Noyes who, while teaching at Princeton in 1916 and temporarily attached to the British Foreign Office as a propagandist, had written of the Casement diaries: "I have seen them and they touch the lowest depths that human degradation has ever touched. Page after page of his diary would be an insult to a pig's trough to let the foul record touch it."[21] In his disclaimer to the *Irish Press*, Noyes insisted that at the time of his 1916 article he saw no need for questioning the authenticity of the diaries (copies of which were freely circulated by the British Home Office), and that aside from the above quoted statement he had said nothing else against Casement.[22] Accepting Noyes's disclaimer, on 13 February 1937 Yeats published in the *Irish Press* a letter and a revised draft of the ballad with Noyes's name left out.[23]

Who is the second person "denounced by name" in the draft of the poem sent to the *Irish Times* and mentioned in Yeats's 28 November letter to Dorothy Wellesley? Though the manuscripts of the Yeats-Wellesley correspondence seem to be lost, a reasonable conjecture can be made from evidence in the published letters.

On 1 December 1936 Dorothy Wellesley pleaded with Yeats: "Please don't insist on this savage attack on _____ at Oxford. Let us find out the facts first."[24] In his reply of 4 December, Yeats continued his denunciation of one of the two figures: "_____ belongs to a type of man for whom I have no respect. Such men have no moral sense. They are painted cardboard manipulated by intreaguers [sic]."[25] On 7 December, however, he wrote: "I am upset & full of remorse. You were quite right. I have wronged _____, though not _____. I got in a blind rage & only half read the passage that excited it. . . . I lost the book & trusted to memory. I am full of shame."[26]

Recalling this exchange of letters but not observing carefully the dates involved, John Unterecker identifies the object of Yeats's "savage attack" as Noyes.[27] It seems unlikely, however, that after asking Dorothy Wellesley twice (7 and 9 December)[28] to burn the letter in which he made his unwarranted accusation, Yeats, now "full of remorse," would two months later (on 2 February) proceed to publish the poem with Noyes's name still mentioned.[29]

I would suggest that the other man "denounced by name" in the 28 November letter, calumniated in the version of the ballad sent to the *Irish Times* in the latter part of November, and discussed further in the correspondence of 1, 4, and 7 December, is Gilbert Murray. Murray, who sided against Casement in 1916, is mentioned a number of times in *The Forged Casement Diaries*. For example, Maloney (p. 61) mentions Murray's article, "Shall Sir Roger Casement Hang?" (written for the 30 July 1916 issue of the *Providence Journal*), and also (p. 226) a *New York Times* interview of 4 August 1916 (the day after Casement was hanged) headlined "Murray Defends Casement's Execution." With Murray identified as the figure in question, a seeming non sequitur in Yeats's 4 December letter makes sense: "However I hate 'Leagues of Nations' & Leagues of all kinds & am not likely to be just."[30] For Murray was Chairman of the League of Nations Union (1923–1938) and President of the League of Nations Committee of Intellectual Cooperation (1928–1940). Moreover, in her letter of 1 December, Dorothy Wellesley places the figure "at Oxford." Quite understandably, Yeats wanted to have his ballad "sung by Irish undergraduates at Oxford" because Murray, Regius Professor of Greek at Oxford until 1936, was there.

"My poetry all comes from rage or lust," Yeats explained to Dorothy Wellesley,[31] and he subsequently sent her a quatrain eventually published (with minor changes) as "The Spur":

> *You think it horrible that lust and rage*
> *Should dance attention upon my old age;*
> *They were not such a plague when I was young;*
> *What else have I to spur me into song?*

Yeats's reaction to these public events is but one manifestation of a more general attitude of "rage" evident in his late years.

Ribh, we recall, studied hatred diligently because it was a cathartic passion that he could dominate and direct. Thus Auden, always mindful of the sense of Yeats's poetry, remarks:

To get the Last Poems of Yeats,
You need not mug up on dates;
All a reader requires
Is some knowledge of gyres
And the sort of people he hates.[32]

Friends and acquaintances almost uniformly mention his quick temper and growing impatience. Certainly, his last poems reveal a man more willing to place himself in direct contact with his "themes," more inclined to strip his matter to bare fundamentals. An old man, and craving "an eagle mind" proper to the old, Yeats recalls mad Timon—"the fury of intelligence baffled and shut in by circumjacent stupidity"[33]—and reminds us of raging Lear—"Off, off, you lendings."

One thinks also of Swift, "beating on his breast in sibylline frenzy blind/Because the heart in his blood-sodden breast had dragged him down into mankind." "The last passion of the Renaissance," Yeats called it. One thinks also of the *saeva indignatio* of "the greatest epitaph in history" that he dared to imitate both in his life and in his work:[34]

Ubi saeva indignatio
Ulterius cor lacerare nequit.
Avi viator
Et imitare si poteris,
Strenuum pro virili libertatis vindicem.

Scanning chaotic scenes everywhere, in his last prose work Yeats declared: "Instead of hierarchical society, where all men are different, came democracy; instead of a science which had rediscovered Anima Mundi . . . came materialism: all that Whiggish world Swift stared on till he became a raging man."[35] "I am fighting in those ballads for what I have been fighting all my life, it is our Irish fight though it has nothing to do with this or that country," he told Dorothy Wellesley. "We remember . . . that our ancestor Swift has gone where 'fierce indignation can lacerate his heart no more,' & we go stark, staring mad."[36] But, as Auden said, "Mad Ireland hurt you into poetry."

Older and more Irish than Swift, in "The Old Stone Cross" a Celtic warrior rages against modern times and its piddling ways:

> *A statesman is an easy man,*
> *He tells his lies by rote;*
> *A journalist makes up his lies*
> *And takes you by the throat;*
> *So stay at home and drink your beer*
> *And let the neighbours vote,*
> > Said the man in the golden breastplate
> > Under the old stone Cross.

His well-tempered breastplate, emblematic both of the man and of the golden times that bred him, not only protects a heart stouter than our lean times will allow, but with that heart scornfully opposes everything "Whiggish" and unrefined. As in "The Statues," we find here Cuchulain-like "calculation, number, measurement"—a trinity of virtues proper to Ireland's "ancient sect"—resolutely set against the "formless spawning fury" of contemporary corruption. Thus, "If Folly link with Elegance/No man knows which is which." Such men, upholding the "upright" values of unfashionable times, preserve (in the Celtic manner) their heroic postures even in the grave. They and their living counterparts figure in "The Black Tower," Yeats's last poem:

> *There in the tomb stand the dead upright,*
> *But winds come up from the shore:*
> *They shake when the winds roar,*
> *Old bones upon the mountain shake.*[37]

"Measurement began our might," Yeats repeats in "Under Ben Bulben," but as gyres ran on, he adds, "Confusion fell upon our thought."

When Yeats sent Ethel Mannin the first of his raging Casement poems he leveled his fire at other ignoble things as well: "Why should I trouble about communism, fascism, liberalism, radicalism, when all . . . are going downstream with the artificial unity which ends every civilization? . . . My rage and that of others like me seems more important—though we may but be the first of the final destroying horde."[38] A few days later, when he sent her "The Spur," he added: "I hate more than you do, for my hatred can have no expression in action. I am a forerunner of that horde that will some day come down the mountains."[39] In "Three Marching Songs," faithful to the trust of "all those renowned generations"—buried men in golden breastplates and "oathbound" defenders of black towers, as well as later worthies such as Emmet

and Parnell—this "mighty" mounted horde seems unwilling to
bide its time any longer:

> *What marches down the mountain pass?*
> *No, no, my son, not yet;*
> *That is an airy spot,*
> *And no man knows what treads the grass.*

✗ In "Under Ben Bulben," where they cast cold eyes on mere
polarities of life and death, Yeats again parades the "unearthly
stuff" of this "indomitable" troop of "Irishry." Again hailing "the
superhuman," Yeats sends his supermen (like Cuchulain) to
"break the flood," to ride herd on contemporary chaos everywhere.

That is what "Three Songs to the One Burden" is all about—
the recollection of an old order now passed away, and the hope
of its restoration. Although the widely different figures of the
three songs seem to have little in common, actually they share a
common memory and are united in a common purpose. As beg-
garman, gentleman, and artist, they are grouped in a favorite
Yeatsian series. All of them, looking far back to greater days, are
working for (though they may not know it) a new world to
come—an Irish "Day of Jubilee," so to speak, when the present
rule of the rabblement will be annihilated by the descent of an
heroic horde come to re-establish integrating order. Thus the
common refrain that unites the three songs: *"From mountain to
mountain ride the fierce horsemen."*

For the moment, forgetting wholes, let us consider parts and
ponder Mannion, "The Roaring Tinker" of the first song, who,
like the burden itself, presents an arresting figure. Though descended from the sea god Manannan mac Lir, he has sunk to
haunts and activities ill-befitting his noble lineage. Yet, conscious
of his ancestry, he is a staunch spokesman for "aristocratic" ways,
so much so that he seems to have dedicated himself to purifying
the blood of others—"Throw likely couples into bed/And knock
the others down." We have good reason to associate him with
Yeats himself, who (so that God would "fill the cradles right")
was at this time busily sounding off on eugenics, selective breed-
ing, and military togetherness ("Armament comes next to edu-
cation. . . . The formation of military families should be encour-
aged."), and on their refreshing results.[40] In his "Farewell to
Yeats" a friend recalled:

Latterly he talked much about eugenics. One would not have expected him to urge a biological remedy for the improvement of the
human race; but he was impressed by the power given by the stupid
to the mediocre, and the mass-production of mediocrity, and had
been listening eagerly to the arguments for biological selection. The
Italians and the Germans were concentrating on sheer numbers; let
us think only of the *quality* of the race. I think it was for this reason
that he favoured what he was constantly talking of as the "unification"
of the State, under an aristocratic order capable of guiding society
out of the dangers of herd thought. He was not easy to follow when
he got off on one of those topics, nor easily to be diverted.[41]

Whatever the analogy, it is clear than Mannion, a good Nietz-
schean, is driven by a lusty will to power, and that like his "strong
farmer" friend John Kinsella (*"What shall I do for pretty girls/
Now my old bawd is dead?"*), he too lustily laments "the shortness of life and changing times."[42] Further, associating his ad-
vancing years with loss of power, and loss of power with dis-
unified being, Mannion longs not only for the resurrection of
the son of Lir, but also for a renewal ("Could that old god rise
up again") of his own sexual potency. Godlike, in the restored
good times he and Crazy Jane would not only "throw likely
couples into bed," but, propagating heartily, would set the pace
as well.

The second song is set, appropriately enough, in Sligo, home
of Ben Bulben and Knocknarea, the mountains around which the
"fierce horsemen" gallop. Home also of Yeats's eccentric hermit
cousin Henry Middleton, "the whole neighbourhood is 'airy':
perhaps because of the battlefields that the conformation of the
ground has determined through the centuries, perhaps because
the fresh and the salt waters from the mountains and the estuary
meet so violently and quickly there."[43] Having seen perhaps
more than his share of worldly "devil's trade," this recluse is de-
termined, like Candide, to cultivate nothing but his own garden.
Though his outer garb is of the latest style, what really keeps him
warm is the memory of a bygone era and the substantial people
who made it "strong." In a disordered world progressively made
more degenerate by its disorderly inhabitants, his private duty
is clear: perfect the individual life; set for one's self the example
of absolute self-sufficiency; do only what is truly essential, and
do that well. Though the young—in one another's arms as well

as at each other's throats—cannot go "straight," by an heroic act of will old Henry Middleton, scion of "half legendary men," can discover mysterious power and wisdom in the straitened circumstances of simple life. Like Shelley's seaside dweller and "Old Rocky Face" of "The Gyres," this old man seems destined to survive "cycles of generation and of ruin." And, as the hoofbeats ring in our ears as they do around the mountains, we might wonder also if, like Ahasuerus and Old Rocky Face, "from his eye looks forth/A life of unconsumèd thought which pierces/ The Present, and the Past, and the To-come."

The third song, Irish even to the point of its traditional "Come all ye" invocation ("Come gather round me players all:/Come praise Nineteen-Sixteen"), returns us to more familiar ground and roundly concludes the cycle, for in James Connolly and the other Easter martyrs we see combined the differing attributes— energy and dream, violence and reflection—of Mannion and Middleton.

The significant achievement common to all the figures of the three songs, we now note, is the triumph of the individual will, "the heroic cry in the midst of despair."[44] Though in this poem we are once again asked to admire those "players" who "resigned" their parts in the "casual comedy" of humdrum living, we too are now addressed as actors called to higher roles. Only ordinary life is played out on a restricting stage, Yeats says throughout the songs; for expansive existence we must abandon mundane props of thought and beguiling "painted" scenes. Having met Mannion, Middleton, and the Easter heroes, we are now invited to attune ourselves to the transcendental pitch of the liberating burden, the "airy" image that motivates them all to higher destinies.

Finally, what of the horsemen? If we conceive of the mountains as forming a circle (as tradition and the sense of both the sentence and the poem would encourage), we apprehend the horsemen as images not only of "fierce" dedication and heroic action, but of the "mighty" completeness of "Truth" as well. Cosmic in its sweeping vision, this prophetic poem reminds us in many ways that Greek *kosmos* means "the world as an ordered whole." Their chase, then, suggests that this "Truth," like time (which Plato in his *Timaeus* called "a moving image of eternity"), not only marches (or gallops) on, but that because of its perfected state assumes the harmonious wholeness of impressive circularity. And just as these horsemen provide us with an emblem of unrelenting pursuit of fundamental verities and of the shape of these verities, so too their configuration reveals analogically the state to which all men and nations must aspire.

Occasionally, Yeats brings together in a single poem many of the themes that pervade the varied creations of his last years. Such a poem is "The Curse of Cromwell," a moving ballad built in "the foul rag-and-bone shop" of an aching heart. Here, motifs of dislocation, disillusionment, degeneration, defeat, and death grow out of the speaker's vision of evil. "It is very poignant because it was my own state watching romance & nobility disappear," Yeats observed.[45] Determined, he would withstand, perhaps transcend. Yet the burden, ambivalent, continues to carry all:

> You ask what I have found, and far and wide I go:
> Nothing but Cromwell's house and Cromwell's murderous crew,
> The lovers and the dancers are beaten into the clay,
> And the tall men and the swordsmen and the horsemen,
>   where are they?
> And there is an old beggar wandering in his pride—
> His fathers served their fathers before Christ was crucified.
>   O what of that, O what of that,
>   What is there left to say?
>
>   .   .   .
>
> But there's another knowledge that my heart destroys,
> As the fox in the old fable destroyed the Spartan boy's,
> Because it proves that things both can and cannot be;
> That the swordsmen and the ladies can still keep company,
> Can pay the poet for a verse and hear the fiddle sound,
> That I am still their servant though all are underground.
>   O what of that, O what of that,
>   What is there left to say? [46]

Once again spurred into song by *saeva indignatio* ("I am expressing my rage against the intelligentsia by writing about Oliver Cromwell who was the Lennin [sic] of his day"[47]), Yeats concludes by alluding, perhaps, to pathetic Gulliver: "And when I pay attention I must out and walk/Among the dogs and horses that understand my talk."[48] But more important here is a more familiar mask, that of the wandering beggar-man, the lonely country poet singing for "the book of the people." "I speak through the mouth of some wandering peasant poet in Ireland," he said while writing the poem,[49] and shortly afterward declared: "I can put my own thought, despair perhaps from the study of present circumstance in the light of ancient philosophy, into the mouth of rambling poets of the seventeenth century . . . and the deeper my thought the more credible, the more peasant-like are ballad singer and rambling poet."[50]

Sung by guests at two Irish Academy of Letters banquets, and chanted over the B.B.C., "The Curse of Cromwell" (ranked by him as among the two best poems he had written for some time[51]) reflects Yeats's eagerness to regain his youthful "power of moving the common man." To do so, to write poems that would "go into the general memory," Yeats seems to have turned to "old Gaelic ballads friends translated to me," as indeed he acknowledged he had done with "The Curse of Cromwell."[52]

Throughout his long career Yeats frequently worked with themes from folklore and literature, but only during the early 1930s did his poetry begin to show in its tone and texture the strong influence of "the rambling poets" of the seventeenth and eighteenth centuries. Much of this influence is attributable to his association with F. R. Higgins and Frank O'Connor. Higgins, a gifted musician, poet, and translator as well as managing director of the Abbey Theatre, collaborated with Yeats in 1935 on the monthly broadsides issued by the Cuala Press.[53] O'Connor, who made his reputation as a short-story writer, for a while devoted himself to the translation of Gaelic verse. In 1936 Yeats commented: "John Synge brought back masculinity to Irish verse with his harsh disillusionment, and later, when the folk movement seemed to support vague political mass excitements, certain poets began to create passionate masterful personality. We remembered the Gaelic poets of the seventeenth and early eighteenth centuries wandering, after the flight of the Catholic nobility, among the boorish and the ignorant, singing their loneliness and their rage; James Stephens, Frank O'Connor made them symbols of our pride."[54] Yeats not only applauded O'Connor's work but contributed active assistance as well. Enthusiastic over these "bare and elegantly functional verses,"[55] Yeats went so far as to suggest revisions for some of O'Connor's already distinguished translations.[56] O'Connor says: "Wild horses could not have kept Yeats from helping with them, and sometimes, having supplied some felicitous line of his own, he promptly stole it back for one of

his original poems. Hence the 'influence' of these poems on Yeats's
later work which Professor William York Tindall has pointed
out."[57]

In "The Curse of Cromwell," for example, Yeats borrowed an
important line from a poem by Egan O'Rahilly (ca. 1670–1726),
whom he saw as "the last voice of feudalism";[58] making things
more felicitous, he made both poet and line his own—"His fathers
served their fathers before Christ was crucified":

> *I shall not call for help until they coffin me—*
> *What good for me to call when hope of help is gone?*
> *Princes of Munster who would have heard my cry*
> *Will not rise from the dead because I am alone.*
>
> .   .   .
>
> *Now I shall cease, death comes, and I must not delay*
> *   By Laune and Laine and Lee, diminished of their pride,*
> *I shall go after the heroes, ay, into the clay—*
> *   My fathers followed theirs before Christ was crucified.*[59]

Like Yeats, many of these Gaelic poets show concern for the
fall of great houses and all they stood for. Again from O'Rahilly:

> *That royal Cashel is bare of house and guest,*
> *That Brian's turreted home is the otter's nest,*
> *That the kings of the land have neither land nor crown*
> *Has made me a beggar before you, Valentine Brown.*[60]

"Foxes round churchyards bare/Gnawing the guts of men," observed a ninth-century ironist.[61]

Lamentation for the passing of "beautiful lofty things," ex-
tended metaphors of decay, images of fiddle music and dance—
familiar Yeatsian motifs—coalesce in "Kilcash." No wonder it
was one of Yeats's favorites, and one to which he contributed "a
good deal of his work."[62] Though Yeats was descended from
Butlers, he did not know that Kilcash was the ancestral home of
one branch of that family:

> *What shall we do for timber?*
> *   The last of the woods is down.*
> *Kilcash and the house of its glory*
> *   And the bell of the house are gone,*
> *The spot where that lady waited*
> *   Who shamed all women for grace*
> *When earls came sailing to greet her*
> *   And Mass was said in the place.*

My grief and my affliction
      Your gates are taken away,
Your avenue needs attention,
      Goats in the garden stray.
The courtyard's filled with water
      And the great earls where are they?
The earls, the lady, the people
      Beaten into the clay.[63]

The question of sources and influences is always a tricky one. Nevertheless, a comparison of "Grania" and Yeats's "Lullaby" reveals definite correspondence, even without benefit of O'Connor's statement that his translation "was the basis" of Yeats's poem, "which he wrote after reading my first version of the poem."[64] Other poems recall Crazy Jane, the Wild Old Wicked Man (*"Daybreak and a candle-end"*), and other *personae* of this period. To quote only from "The Old Woman of Beare," "Growing Old," and "Retirement":

It is pay
And not men ye love today,
But when we were young, ah, then
We gave all our hearts to men.

　　　・　　・　　・

'Tis not age that makes my pain
But the eye that sees so plain
How when all it loves decays
Femuin's ways are gold again.

Woman full of wile
      Take your hand away,
Nothing tempts me now,
      Sick for love you pray.

　　　・　　・　　・

Your twined branching hair,
      Your grey eye dew-bright,
Your rich rounded breast
      Turn to lust the sight.

> *In youth I served my time*
> *To kissing and love-making;*
> *Now that I must retire*
> *I feel my heart is breaking.*
>
> .   .   .
>
> *And memory makes a torment*
> *Of all my past blisses—*
> *Ah, God, ah God! 'tis food today*
> *That feeds me and not kisses.*[65]

Knowing these translations, and knowing what we know of
Yeats's relationship to them, we may safely agree that "here, too,
he found congenial manner, congenial tone."[66] These rich poems
stand sharply in the background of the stirring fifth section of
Yeats's testament, "Under Ben Bulben":

> *Irish poets, learn your trade,*
> *Sing whatever is well made,*
> *Scorn the sort now growing up*
> *All out of shape from toe to top,*
> *Their unremembering hearts and heads*
> *Base-born products of base beds.*
> *Sing the peasantry, and then*
> *Hard-riding country gentlemen,*
> *The holiness of monks, and after*
> *Porter-drinkers' randy laughter;*
> *Sing the lords and ladies gay*
> *That were beaten into the clay*
> *Through seven heroic centuries;*
> *Cast your mind on other days*
> *That we in coming days may be*
> *Still the indomitable Irishry.*

Certainly, to understand and appreciate fully this "bitter and
gay" period of Yeats's career, we must turn to the "heroic mood"
of other days, and say of him as an eighth-century poet said of
hard times, "Tempest on the plain of Lir/Bursts its barriers far
and near."[67]

CHAPTER SIX ❋ TIMES OF GLORY

The old order, gone or passing away, the aged Yeats was de-termined not to let go unsung. Though "the meaning of all song" is that all things pass away, what is sung about endures in the "deep heart's core" of the singer. "In the foul rag-and-bone shop of the heart," where all the "ladders" of ascension rise, Yeats, again recalling "heart-mysteries," found fresh images of vanished times.

"The Municipal Gallery Revisited," though in one sense an enumeration of "old themes," through a brilliant series of sharp images demonstrating how "things both can and cannot be" proves nevertheless that there was much "left to say" of Ireland's irreplaceable "tall men" now gone "underground." Clearly "still their servant," Yeats in this poem becomes a pilgrim before their pictured presence. Sacramental, their portraits (outward signs of "a greater, a more gracious time") become instruments for the miraculous transformation to which the poem moves. Though in the fourth and fifth stanzas these ghostly images bring him to his knees and to simultaneous states of devotion and despair, by the end of the poem, as the motif of rootedness takes firmer hold, they enable him to rejoice. These powerfully associative images, not only limning his friends and Ireland's history but symbolizing his career as well, become so heavily charged and intertwined that they lead him ultimately to an even more overpowering realization—the awareness that the "glory" he senses in the gallery is the greater glory of all. Like the "great-rooted blossomer," proud nation, noble friends, and inspired labor grow into one.

Though a cursory reading might leave the impression that the poem is loosely constructed, consisting in the main of a rambling series of associatively recalled vignettes of a dozen or so figures of widely varying sorts, analysis of the whole and explication of its parts shows it to be logically conceived and ordered as well as carefully developed and sustained. Central to theme and form here is the principle of antithesis, which not only underlies Yeats's total conception, but which acts as well as the guiding principle of development and progression. From beginning to end, antithetical pairs and sets of images, and antithesis within a single image, create a network of tensions largely responsible for the highly charged tone maintained throughout the poem's wide and frequent oscillations.

Immediately after the formal opening of the first line, anonymous "ambush" (John Keating's painting "The Men of the West") and anonymous "pilgrims at the waterside" (John Lavery's "Saint Patrick's Purgatory") metaphorically define and establish opposing states which we discover more concretely in each of the specific persons mentioned thereafter. From the very beginning the connotations presented constitute the type for all that is yet to come, for informing this antithetical pair of images (with its overtones of dusty roads and still waters, abrupt death and life eternal) are hints of outward movement and inward gaze, uprooting and deep-rootedness, chaos and tradition, war and peace, guilt and redemption, pride and humility, and perhaps even many-facing power and glory, the dominant note on which the poem comes to a measured but triumphant close.

Roger Casement, Arthur Griffith, and Kevin O'Higgins (recalled in three paintings by John Lavery), three strong-willed and tough-minded historical figures emblematic of the turbulent public life of Yeats's time, in the name of high principle stirred troubled waters in their revolutionary pursuit of violent political ends. Their secular pilgrimage, full of sound and fury, was either frustrated or only partially completed; for two of them, it led the way to cruel and dusty death.

Casement, a man of divided loyalties who stubbornly remained loyal to his conception of right, nobly served imperial Britain; yet, after he was knighted, he came to conspire against that land whose dominion over Ireland and himself he decried and denied. The nobility of his famous speech from the dock and the dignity of his bearing on the gallows contrast violently with the baseness of the infamous writings attributed to him and the even more appalling possibility of their genuineness.[1] As British consul he brought to light outrage after outrage and freed Congolese and Putamayan natives from inhuman treatment; yet his portrait and its setting ("The Court of Criminal Appeal") must show the inhuman circumstances of a man ambushed by fate, "upon trial, half-hidden by the bars,/Guarded."

Arthur Griffith, whose stare of "hysterical pride" is compounded of contrasting elements, in Yeats's eyes sometimes worked for opposing ends. Though in 1899 he defended *The Countess Cathleen*, offering to bring "a lot of men from the Quays" who would "applaud anything the Church did not like," eight years later this Sinn Fein leader sent "the little clubs" out to jeer Synge's *Playboy*.[2] Without culture, Yeats told Lady Gregory, "men like Griffith . . . can renounce external things . . . but not envy, revenge, jealousy and so on. I wrote a note a couple of years ago in which I compared Griffith and his like to the Eunuchs in Ricketts's picture watching Don Juan ride through Hell."[3] Though he indirectly pleaded Yeats's cause by urging his good friend John MacBride not to marry Maud Gonne, this influential editor angered Yeats by his attacks on Synge, Hugh Lane, the Abbey Theatre, and Yeats's work. Because he held that "literature should be subordinate to nationalism," it is not surprising that Yeats long deplored his influence on the Irish mind; convinced that literature "must have its own ideal," Yeats wanted to challenge Griffith to a debate on "our two policies."[4] "Yeats could never forgive Griffith . . . or think of him as other than a fanatic," we are told.[5] Yet this same man, imprisoned by the British, could tell the Governor of Gloucester Jail that the Irishmen there "would require special facilities on June 13th, as it was the birthday of their national poet."[6] In this poem his nationalistic "hysterical pride" stands in antithesis to the solid, earthy pride of Lady Gregory and John Synge, who, searching for a nation's roots, labored to shape its national identity.

Kevin O'Higgins, Vice-President of the Executive Council of the Dail and according to Yeats "the finest intellect in Irish public life,"[7] was ambushed outside his home by gunmen. "A great man in his pride/Confronting murderous men," Yeats wrote ("Death") of the death of the man whom he looked upon as "Parnell's successor."[8] Yet, as the stark contrast between the "gentle questioning look" of his countenance and his soul's incapacity for "remorse or rest" indicates, O'Higgins was a violently divided man. A sensitive intellectual, in a speech to the Dail he called for the blood of Erskine Childers, a scapegoat executed on the sole charge of possessing a toy pistol (ironically, one given him by Michael Collins, the enemy leader) fastened to his braces by a safety pin.[9] (Convicted late in the evening of 23 November 1922 after a trial remarkably similar to Casement's, Childers was shot at dawn the following day before an appeal could be made. "Even in England this execution was held by jurists to be a judicial murder. . . . His execution excited grief, anger and shame."[10]) In the name of authority and the establishment of the rule of law, O'Higgins actively promoted the shooting of jailed prisoners. Tugged to extremes, this strange figure, while attempting in a speech before the Dail to justify the reprisal execution of his close friend Rory O'Connor and three other political prisoners, wept in public for the only time in his life.[11]

The impersonal but concrete images of the "revolutionary soldier kneeling to be blessed" and the priest "with an upraised hand/Blessing the Tricolour," recalling and extending further the images in the second line ("ambush," "pilgrims at the waterside"), frame the first stanza of the poem and develop its theme more fully. We have here not only antithetically constructed analogues for the divided lives of the public men mentioned previously, but a metaphorical expression of Ireland's recent public character, where church and state, revolutionary power and vested authority, form an unholy but popular alliance.[12] And looking ahead to the fourth, fifth, and sixth stanzas, we see here also the two dominant elements which, when yoked together, within Yeats's lifetime toppled the Anglo-Irish Ascendancy.

Each of these two figures (inspired by John Lavery's "The Blessing of the Colours") is basically antithetical: we note a soldier, perhaps on his way to or from an ambush, "surrendering"; and a representative of ecclesiastical authority, perhaps confusing

Caesar and Christ, blessing the green, white, and orange flag presented to the Young Ireland Movement a century earlier by republican, anticlerical Frenchmen.[13] Juxtaposed, the two figures ironically form a paradoxical image: we note antitheses of "down" (genuflection) and "up" (blessing), guerrilla and hierarch, new and old.

Much of the theme and technique of this section is reminiscent of "Easter 1916," another evocation of men who with tragically "enchanted" hearts "troubled the living stream" of history. Casement, Griffith, and O'Higgins—they too are now recorded in Yeats's memory as men who brought "excess of love" to the terrible and bewildering pursuit of imagined ideals.[14] "This is not the dead Ireland of my youth," Yeats says of their transfigured times, "but an Ireland/The poets have imagined, terrible and gay." "Imagined" suggests at once the poet's ordered re-creation of experience (such as this poem itself), the practical results of impractical art ("Did that play of mine send out/Certain men the English shot?"), and the quixotic possibility that bitter actuality may have been but a dream of life.

The third stanza focuses on Major Robert Gregory, Hugh Lane, and Hazel Lavery, who in company with the political figures just seen are emblematic of frustrated ends, only partially fulfilled destinies. Like the above-mentioned political men, these figures are all associated with controversies of various sorts. On the other hand, though incomplete, they are to be esteemed for their gracious natures and magnanimous acts. In this sense they anticipate Lady Gregory, the grandest of them all. Two of them, we observe, are denoted in terms of their relationship to Yeats's patroness: "son," "her sister's son." The third, Hazel Lavery, figures here not only because her painter husband's work is amply represented in the gallery, two of them ("Hazel Lavery at Her Easel" and "It is Finished," a deathbed scene) providing Yeats with the "living and dying" image, but also because of her friendship with Lady Gregory and the common cause they made in trying to recover the Lane paintings. The branches of the Gregory tree, we note, embracing Synge and Yeats, are evident in this poem as well.

Abortively ended, the relatively short but finely balanced life of Robert Gregory is marked by the tragic contrast between all he embodied and all he could never do. (A talented painter him-

self, he is recalled in the gallery by Charles Shannon's portrait.)
And his cousin Hugh Lane, who "joined the profession of a
picture-dealer with the magnanimity of a Medici,"[15] by the ironical fact of an unwitnessed codicil to his will was prevented from
donating his paintings to a city whose Biddys and Paudeens had
scorned them while the paintings were still in Dublin.[16] "There
is something heroic and pathetic in this old importunate widow
begging at this doorstep and at that," says Lennox Robinson of
Lady Gregory's fifteen-year struggle to reclaim her nephew's
paintings.[17]

It is evident, then, that the first three stanzas, though divided
into two groups, share a common antithetical understructure:
the contrast between what the figures dreamed and expected, and
what they had to settle for. Surely this is one of the reasons why
Yeats, "heart-smitten with emotion," had to "sink down,/My
heart recovering with covered eyes." As in "Easter 1916," however, "We know their dream; enough/To know they dreamed
and are dead." Because each of them, like Casement, "did what
he had to do," their "living and dying" is lifted to epic stature.
In the gallery portraits, in Yeats's consciousness, and in the poem
before us, their "tale" is now offered to all "as though some
ballad-singer had sung it all."

If it is meet that a ballad simile should close the first movement,
it is equally right that it should anticipate the next group of
stanzas, for it is here that Yeats turns to his own work and to
the ground from which it arose. The strong tensions and sharp
juxtapositions characteristic of balladry not only underscore what
he has just finished setting forth, but, along with other ballad
techniques, characterize much of his best verse, especially that of
his last years when "with impediments plain to all" he longed to
sing "with the ancient simplicity."[18] "Ancient simplicity" he
found, too, in John Synge, who (after a sojourn in the Aran
Islands) made it a specialty; and in proud and humble Lady
Gregory, who collected old tales and young poets. From now to
the end of the poem they stand on either side of Yeats, as they
literally do in the second line of stanza six ("John Synge, I and
Augusta Gregory") and as they did on the occasion of his lecture
to the Swedish Royal Academy when he won the Nobel Prize
for 1923:

"When your King gave me medal and diploma, two forms should

have stood, one at either side of me, an old woman sinking into the infirmity of age and a young man's ghost. I think when Lady Gregory's name and John Synge's name are spoken by future generations, my name, if remembered, will come up in the talk, and that if my name is spoken first their names will come in their turn because of the years we worked together. I think that both had been well pleased to have stood beside me at the great reception at your Palace, for their work and mine has delighted in history and tradition." I think as I speak these words of how deep down we have gone, below all that is individual, modern and restless, seeking foundations for an Ireland that can only come into existence in a Europe that is still but a dream.[19]

The fifth stanza, lacking a line, looks back to times of wholeness and health:

> My mediaeval knees lack health until they bend,
> But in that woman, in that household where
> Honour had lived so long, all lacking found.
> Childless I thought, "My children may find here
> Deep-rooted things," but never foresaw its end,
> And now that end has come I have not wept;
> No fox can foul the lair the badger swept—

Now, Yeats's "mediaeval knees" must "bend" because he is old and—especially without Lady Gregory's sustaining presence—weak; and also because he is "in despair" that we will never again see her type of "pride" and "humility," seemingly antithetical attributes actually complementary, and descriptive of her unique "excellence."[20] Echoing the image of genuflection in the first two stanzas, this rich metaphor also suggests Yeats's "pilgrim soul" (in the context of his early poems) as well as his posture of feudal devotion.[21]

It suggests filial piety, too, for while Lady Gregory flourished those lacking wholeness could achieve it in her "household," a metaphor not only for "honour" but all else that makes for unity of being. If, reconciling opposites, Coole fostered wholeness (Yeats tells us that "childless" he once foresaw there "deep-rooted" experience for his "children"), so too its passing now reduces everything to vulgar incoherence. In the fifth stanza this condition is expressed in the counterbalancing of "all lacking found" by "its end." However, just as the first two conjunctions ("but," lines two and six) abruptly shifted the mood of his meditation (in both instances the clauses coming before and after thus standing in antithesis), so too the third: *"And* now that end has come," developing "never foresaw its end," is completed by the counterstatement of "I have not wept." Thus, the chiasmus of lines five and six in which opposing elements are balanced is followed by the terse affirmation of the concluding line, "No fox can foul the lair the badger swept," which in itself perfectly effects a balance of strongly opposing elements. Hence we may note that "lair," the fulcrum of this crucial line, not only functions as a metaphorical echo of ravaged Coole, but also establishes it firmly as the courtly "household" of abiding "traditional sanctity and loveliness." The filial piety motif is reinforced by our recollection of Yeats's admiration for Edmund Spenser, whose devotion to the Earl of Leicester he recalled in a 1902 essay: "At the end of a long beautiful passage he laments that unworthy men should be in the dead earl's place, and compares them to the fox—an unclean feeder—hiding in the lair 'the badger swept.' "[22]

"Traditional sanctity and loveliness," the chosen theme of "last romantics" such as Synge, Yeats, and Lady Gregory, are the essential features of "the book of the people" praised in "Coole Park and Ballylee, 1931" and in the sixth stanza of this poem. These values, inherent in the "deep-rooted things" of Coole, must be native to poetry as well. Like that giant wrestler Antaeus (who, as son of Terra, remained invincible so long as he touched the earth), poets who would create vital art must draw their sustenance from "contact with the soil." Just as Antaeus was strangled when held aloft by Hercules, so too—the suggestion follows—the artist who loses this vital contact is made sterile by the technological values of our Herculean machine age. Poetry is made profound and lovely, invincible and proud, only when its roots grow from the "deep down" depths of nourishing tradition, "below all that is . . . modern and restless." This, Yeats tells us, is the "sole test" of value. "The noble and the beggar-man" for whom such verses are written properly preside over the close of the stanza and the second major movement of the poem, for these images, recalling Antaeus (giant, earth), also recall Lady Gregory and Coole ("pride" and "humility").

As for the transition from stanza five to stanza six, Yvor Winters claims that it is "awkward" because "Yeats apparently thought that the line at the end of five needed a footnote, and I dare say it does; but he puts this footnote in parentheses at the beginning of six, and it is unimpressive as poetry, and it detracts from the unity of six."[23] Quite the contrary. The fox/lair/ badger metaphor does not *require* a footnote because it is still comprehensive and effective without any special information as to its source; and the parenthetical opening line of stanza six— ("An image out of Spenser and the common tongue")—certainly does not detract from the unity of the poem. Winters misunderstands its function. This line is eminently successful because it serves a twofold *unifying* function: it points back in the poem to courtly Spenser, whose "tongue" (as we have just seen in the homey metaphor) is laudably "common" and whose inimitable poetry is rooted in the common heritage of our tongue; and it looks ahead to the substance of the stanza, where we learn that the "common tongue" flourishes only in rooted sources, something uncommon in our uncourtly and tawdry day. The parenthetical line, then, is the pivot of the entire poem, the point at which the speaker turns from the portraits in the gallery to his portentous generalizations concerning the great value of "contact with the soil."

Antithetical to the last, Yeats's "dream" does not acknowledge middle ground. "The noble and the beggar-man" is significant also in the sense that, excluding the middle class and its deracinated values, it relegates the nationalist heroes of modern Ireland to a less gigantic level. The context of the sixth stanza, we must remember, is not restricted to poetry; Yeats says "All that we did, all that we said" as well as merely "sang." Thus, "We three alone in modern times," he suggests, have served the highest interests of the nation. Not that Yeats wanted to lord it over Casement, Griffith, O'Higgins, and others. Far from it. Rather, the point here in this stanza and throughout the poem as well is that just as art imitates "life," so too must life imitate "art."

As we might expect from a meditation on the meaning of friendship, devotion forms the all-embracing and unifying theme of the entire poem. The nationalist heroes, the revolutionary soldier, and the clergyman are devoted to abstractions; Augusta Gregory's son, nephew, and friend are devoted to noble deeds; while Lady Gregory herself, quintessentially aristocratic, is nobly devoted to Irish culture and two of its most brilliant ornaments; finally, Synge, Yeats, and Lady Gregory, devoted to each other and adorning everything, are sworn to the gigantic task of defining and achieving the truest type of life and art. Surely, Yeats suggests, this type of devotion makes terrible beauties of us all.

"Ireland not as she is displayed in guide book or history, but Ireland seen because of the magnificent vitality of her painters, in the glory of her passions," was to be the subject of a poem, Yeats announced to a group of friends and patrons at a testimonial banquet held on 17 August 1937 by the Irish Academy of Letters.[24] The terrible gaiety of "that great pictured song" [25] not only reveals an Ireland "imagined" only by artists and poets, but shows as well the norm and the means for achieving such an imaginative revelation. For conclusive evidence we have the final stanza, which, integrating and raising all to mythic dimensions, also illustrates this metamorphic process.

Yeats's conception is clear: just as the political destiny of a nation is (for good or for ill) hammered out in the forge of energetic dedication, so too is the cultural and ideological unity of that nation molded by strenuous devotion to timeless patterns. Likewise, Yeats tells us, does the whole of a man's life rest on an organic arrangement of devoted relationships. Therefore, "You that would judge me, do not judge alone/This book or that. . . ." Rather, judge in the larger context of this complexity of allegiances, this "deep-rooted" tangle of relationships whereby a man's country, his co-workers, and his craft cohere gloriously like the components of some impressive feudal structure.

Moreover, just as the history that these dead men and women of the gallery once made now makes them holy to our remembrance, so too their holy aspect transforms the gallery into a temple, a "hallowed place" for their ghostly and abiding presence. (I read *hallowed place* both as "consecrated," i.e., "holy," and as "sainted," "full of saints," i.e., "inhabited by hallows.") Their story, the story of Yeats's participation in their common enterprise, and the literature created out of both, must be seen and judged as one. In old age, a time to judge and to be judged, Yeats senses that the judgment may be glorious. In its ambiguity, however, the line "Think where man's glory most begins and ends" precludes an easy victory or a facile judgment. While "begins and ends" refers primarily to the totality and wholeness of "man's glory" (its "framed" state, according to the portrait context), it also—echoing the "despair" of stanza four ("I am in despair that time may bring/Approved patterns of women or of men/But not that self-same excellence again") and the "end" of Coole—hints that the times of glory are ended. Nevertheless—and herein rests the triumph—it is clear that the "history" of which Yeats is now an integral part is a glorious one indeed, for the "lineaments" of its "permanent or impermanent images" embody everything that rooted men esteem and must emulate forever.

Remembrance of images from times past, always a favorite activity for Yeats, continues to inform many of his last poems. Whether elegiac or heroic, these poems focused on uncommon men and women scorn common vision for other roads to truth. Often the truth is mythic. If for Crazy Jane and her family the way down is the way out, so too the other way around; for the making of myth, a way of ascension, is a promising road to insight. Heightened perception, the way of the poet, sometimes reveals the tragic grandeur of lone eminences such as The O'Rahilly. Other times, as we have seen in "The Municipal Gallery Revisited" and will see in "Beautiful Lofty Things," it reveals the "whatness" of friends from the "tragic and gay" past. Always, however, Yeats views his subjects in retreating light, seeing them all as "Olympians," fabled things "never known again." Like Astraea fled from the world of men, these "masterful images" now loom large in memory. Constellated there and in the poems themselves, they not only brighten Yeats's old age but illumine as well the recaptured past.

In "Beautiful Lofty Things" Yeats once again shows us a gallery of people who have given meaning to his life with what Proust called "privileged moments." Drawn and exalted in the fury of their arrogant gestures and proud postures, these exquisite objects reflect not only their own unique "excellence" but Yeats's "glory" as well:

My father upon the Abbey stage, before him a raging crowd:
"This Land of Saints," and then as the applause died out,
"Of plaster Saints"; his beautiful mischievous head thrown back.[26]

Yeats's strategy is to catalogue memorable moments of intensity, and to do so as sparely as possible. So intense are these moments that (except for a quotation) the poem does not contain a single sentence. As Yeats adds image to image he underscores the bareness of each phrase by markedly avoiding any type of connective or similar syntactical device. Everything is telescoped between the economical introduction of the first three words and an insistently succinct summation.

Non-discursive as in a painting, these completely presentational structures are intended to embody absolutes of character, so that like their images, the characters portrayed become symbolic. To this end Yeats constructs a set of portrait busts (three of the five figures are described in terms of "head") intended to reveal each of the figures in an arrested, hence enduring gesture. Through the minute we are invited to apprehend the grand; by way of the seemingly ephemeral we are expected to discover the truly lasting. This is so because what dominates is not an isolated fact but the complex character of the man which the single recollection, however ostensibly random, suggestively sums up and epitomizes. Thus, as our consciousness receives these apparently fleeting and insignificant symbolic impressions, both the images presented and the mind recording them become enlarged. "Character," absolutely "isolated by a deed," here truly is intended to "engross the present and dominate memory."[27] Just as for Proust these heightened moments of insight into the thingness of the thing redeemed time itself, so too for Joyce, Yeats, and other modern writers they make for "sudden spiritual manifestation."[28] Though Joyce thought that Yeats was born too late to learn anything from him,[29] it is clear that both savored and recorded "epiphanies."

Spoken at the turn of the century, Standish O'Grady's "high nonsensical words" prophesied terrible times to come: "He stood between two tables, touching one or the other for support, and said in a low penetrating voice: 'We have now a literary movement, it is not very important; it will be followed by a political movement, that will not be very important; then must come a military movement, that will be important indeed.' "[30] This man "at once all passion and all judgment," and others like him, lived long in Yeats's mind.[31] "When I try to recall his physical appearance," Yeats says, "my father's picture in the Municipal Gallery blots out my own memory. He comes before me with a normal robust body, dim obsessed eyes, upon the wall above his head the title of a forgotten novel: *Ye Loste Lande*."[32]

The O'Rahilly,[33] a hero of the prophesied "military movement," was destined to shed his blood for the "holy" "loste lande" of Ireland. Returning to Dublin from Limerick where he had gone on Saturday, 22 April 1916, to cancel arrangements for the distribution of arms lost the previous day when the German freighter *Aud* was trapped and scuttled off Queenstown (Cobh), he learned that plans had been changed once again. Though he thought the Rising was "all a tragic mistake,"[34] he loaded his car with guns and explosives and sped to insurgent headquarters at the Dublin General Post Office, where he is reported to have said: "I have helped to wind up the clock, and must be there to hear it strike."[35] The following Friday, as the Post Office burned, he led the first party out of Pearse's doomed headquarters and was killed by machine gun fire in Moore Lane, where a plaque on the wall now recalls his gallantry.[36]

Yeats's commemorative poem ("The O'Rahilly") asserts mythic truth in the face of recorders of historical judgment. The "polite, meaningless words" of the refrain (*"How goes the weather?"*), though seemingly "nonsensical" (even though they could allude to the bad weather that plagued the inception of the Rising), set off the more the "high" achievement of this untroubled beauty. The bloody Easter passion of this "strikingly handsome young man always dressed in a saffron kilt,"[37] Yeats says, makes of him too "a beautiful lofty thing . . ./Heroically lost, heroically found." Making myth, the O'Rahilly—"isolated by a deed"— himself becomes mythical, because Yeatsian "passion," as Donald Stauffer says, is "the moment of such intensity that it escapes from time and from personality and becomes a part of the common human heritage."[38]

CHAPTER SEVEN ✳ FABULOUS ARTIFICE

W̲ʜᴀᴛ Crazy Jane says "on the Day of Judgment"—

*"Love is all
Unsatisfied
That cannot take the whole
Body and soul"*;
And that is what Jane said—

perhaps goes without saying, but the vexing problem of the integration of body and soul remained for Yeats a major concern up to the last years of his life when he made a final effort to confront questions that had long been fundamental to his art. In "The Three Bushes" and its six attendant lyrics he pondered the familiar antinomy of body and soul and laid bare others equally profound and perplexing: appearance and reality, the many and the one, man and God. Though Yeats's varying and sometimes antithetical postures preclude summary judgment of his final attitudes, I would urge nevertheless that the "Three Bushes" sequence does more than epitomize and dramatize once again Yeats's characteristic vacillation. These deceptively simple poems, I hope to show, are ultimately concerned with the antithetical stresses seen by Yeats throughout his career as central to the

86

human condition. All of them reveal artistically wrought perspectives on the problem of unity of being. And the last two, especially when read in the context of the sequence as a whole, I interpret as suggesting a view of and a reaction to life radically different from what Yeats had presented for many years. In this sense I see the sequence as consonant with other poems of his final period wherein he brought his life's work to wholeness by discovering dimensions and stressing concerns hitherto scorned, ignored, or neglected.[1]

This sequence shows not only the urgency of the aged Yeats's sexual drive, but also the scrupulously honest poet's recognition that even the most dazzling architectonics of the creative imagination, though capable of embodying "artifices of eternity," cannot resolve in any actual sense the conflicts of an all too real world peopled by men and women all too human. This conclusion, a hard one for Yeats especially to reach, is central to an understanding of the final phase of his work. Further, the poems of this sequence are not, as some have suggested, scatological, but eschatological. Embodying one of Yeats's most meaningful meditations on last things, they strengthen the base upon which future discussion of his tragic sense of life must be founded. On grounds of technique, too, these poems should be excluded from the many in Yeats's final volume which John Crowe Ransom judged to "miss the delicate strategy of the imaginative process."[2] Indeed, awareness of their high achievement may help us to see Yeats's often misunderstood last poems in a more favorable light.[3]

During the latter part of 1936, Yeats and Dorothy Wellesley, making plans for the publication of a collection of ballads which they would edit jointly, decided to explore the body and soul theme by writing ballads of their own. The March and September 1937 issues of *Broadsides* contain Yeats's "The Three Bushes" and Lady Gerald's "The Lady, the Squire, and the Serving-Maid,"[4] variations on what Yeats claimed in the subtitle to be "An Incident from the 'Historia mei Temporis' of the Abbé Michel de Bourdeille."[5]

The plot of both narratives is essentially the same. In Yeats's version, the lady, recognizing that love should not lack "its proper food" but unwilling to share her lover's bed because "if I saw

myself creep in/I think I should drop dead," decides to keep her
chastity and yet bring love to fulfillment by sending her chambermaid as her secret replacement. Ignorant of the deception, the
lover is satisfied, and shows it in his high-powered singing and
riding. One day, however, he is thrown from his horse and dies
from the fall; and his lady, because "she loved him with her
soul," perishes from grief. Over their graves the chambermaid
plants two rose bushes

> *That when they had grown large*
> *Seemed sprung from but a single root*
> *So did their roses merge.*
> O my dear, O my dear.

Years later, after confessing to an understanding priest, she too
dies, and is laid on the other side of the lover, where another rose
bush is planted to complete the tangle:

> *And now none living can,*
> *When they have plucked a rose there,*
> *Know where its roots began.*
> O my dear, O my dear.

   This merging of roses invites a symbolic interpretation not
only because in Yeats's poetry the rose almost always suggests
(among other things) "Unity of Being," wholeness, but more
specifically because it here serves as an emblem of the tripartite
consummation engineered by the lady when she plays both ends
against the middle. Though it is still true that "The grave's a fine
and private place,/But none, I think, do there embrace," the
living roses suggest that an embrace of sorts has indeed finally
occurred. (Ironically, the coy lady, who had asserted that if she
crept into her lover's bed she would "drop dead," now "embraces" him in the rosebed of their twin graves.) Moreover, not
only does the wholeness to which love must attain in order to be
kept alive (better, to come alive) come about through deception,
but this wholeness suggested by the twined rose branches is
itself a matter of "deception." The roses and especially the "single
root" from which all of them seem to have sprung function, after
all, not only as a metaphor for sexual wholeness (the integration
of one's body and soul, and the union of two lovers who would
"merge" into one) but also for the satisfying condition—in
Stephen Dedalus's terms, "wholeness, harmony and radiance"—
produced by artful artifice.

Though Yeats began "The Three Bushes" as a *jeu d'esprit*, by
the time he was done with the poem he had become so involved
that he went on to write six songs intended to develop the psychological and metaphysical considerations implicit in his original
theme. These lyrics, individual songs of the lady, lover, and
chambermaid, present angles of vision and modes of response
appropriate to the rationalist, romantic, and realist temperaments
of the three *personae*.

A logic-chopper by nature, the cerebretonic lady ably employs
her art as, true to type, she energetically attempts to resolve on
a purely rational level the difficulty besetting her. Bodily participation in love she will not have, yet unsatisfied with the incompleteness she has chosen, she finds satisfaction in the elegant
artifice her mind is capable of fabricating. Her three songs, moving from blunt statement to measured ratiocination to sophisticated verbal play, eventually lead to resolution; but this resolution
takes place solely on the intellectual level. Her fiction, though
supreme, operates only within the limited universe of the poem
itself.

Love, itself an obsession, obsesses all the more when it is ex-
perienced imperfectly by one who knows what its perfection
entails but who is nevertheless reluctant to permit its consummation because convinced of its essential sinfulness. This is the
theme of "The Lady's First Song":

> *I turn round*
> *Like a dumb beast in a show,*
> *Neither know what I am*
> *Nor where I go,*
> *My language beaten*
> *Into one name;*
> *I am in love*
> *And that is my shame.*
> *What hurts the soul*
> *My soul adores,*
> *No better than a beast*
> *Upon all fours.*

Body, the lady thinks, is bestial, and now that she is in love and
knows that love cannot dispense with body, she irrationally im-
putes this bestiality to her entire being and tortures herself with
consuming feelings of guilt. Though wise and well-integrated

Solomon and Sheba ("Solomon to Sheba") spend all day happily
cutting the world down to size by going "round and round/In
the narrow theme of love/Like an old horse in a pound," this less
enlightened lady, a prisoner of an inhuman separation of body
and soul, is condemned to see herself as shamefully captive in a
frustrating "round" of pointless activity. Her frustrating situation is underscored all the more by the ironical simile she uses
to describe it: she is like a beast on *display* ("show") because of
the *dark secret* she has kept hidden ("dumb").

"The Lady's Second Song" is addressed to the chambermaid:

> *What sort of man is coming*
> *To lie between your feet?*
> *What matter, we are but women.*
> *Wash; make your body sweet;*
> *I have cupboards of dried fragrance,*
> *I can strew the sheet.*
> The Lord have mercy upon us.
>
> *He shall love my soul as though*
> *Body were not at all,*
> *He shall love your body*
> *Untroubled by the soul,*
> *Love cram love's two divisions*
> *Yet keep his substance whole.*
> The Lord have mercy upon us.
>
> *Soul must learn a love that is*
> *Proper to my breast,*
> *Limbs a love in common*
> *With every noble beast.*
> *If soul may look and body touch,*
> *Which is the more blest?*
> The Lord have mercy upon us.

In this poem and the next we see the lady ingeniously attempting
to rationalize her way out of her predicament. She has two problems to solve. First, she must see that the lover, who needs body
as well as soul, is satisfied; for if he is not, love will die, and with
it the chance that she may be loved for her soul alone. Second,
she must convince herself that she *can* be loved for her soul alone,
that body and soul can separately participate in love, and that
each alone, loved, may be brought to fulfillment. Although, recognizing the function of her sex, she says "What matter, we are

but women," she herself is unwilling to become a whole woman. Rather, wholeness she will create by deception, through the agency of an alter ego. Thus, immediately after saying "we" in line three, she says "Wash; make . . ." and "I have . . . I can . . . ," thereby setting "you" and "I" apart. Also, preparing us for her final song, she elaborates on the distinction just made by assigning the upper part of her body to the soul, and the lower, bestial part to the body of her alter ego. By means of projection, therefore, she is able to disengage herself from troubling body and thus can now speak of "beast" as "noble." Now, also, it would seem, the unknowing lover will love two apart while thinking that he possesses two in one. In the daylight, presumably, he will love the lady's soul in a chaste "daytime" way, as though body did not exist at all—so the lady wants to believe; and in the depths of night, oblivious to the purer claims of more exalted and enlightened soul, he will probe and possess the body of a secret other.

Whereas the first song showed the lady hopelessly lost, the second finds her saved thanks to her skillful construction of a hopeful paradox. Body and soul, like the rose cluster of "The Three Bushes," she has arranged to be one and many at the same time. No wonder, then, the priestly cast of the refrain, *"The Lord have mercy upon us."* This response, a comment offered by both the lady and the reader, asks at once that awesome transformation and brainy guile be praised, and that these deceptions be forgiven.

The third song, one of Yeats's most accomplished lyrics, is the lady's masterpiece:

> *When you and my true lover meet*
> *And he plays tunes between your feet,*
> *Speak no evil of the soul,*
> *Nor think that body is the whole,*
> *For I that am his daylight lady*
> *Know worse evil of the body;*
> *But in honour split his love*
> *Till either neither have enough,*
> *That I may hear if we should kiss*
> *A contrapuntal serpent hiss,*
> *You, should hand explore a thigh,*
> *All the labouring heavens sigh.*

Again addressing herself to the chambermaid, the lady continues to insist on division, but does so here in order to establish the terms of integration worked out in the concluding lines. Sundered body and soul she impressively brings together while actually keeping them apart. We note that, as in the previous poem, here too in the opening lines pronoun use is shifty: although the lady says *"my* true lover," this lover is to lie "between *your* feet." All the antinomies—day and night, upper and lower, breast and limb, soul and body—are implicit in the "split" love which the lady urges. The grand illusion of wholeness to which the poem moves comes about through the lady's mental agility. Only by verbal magic, so to speak, is she able to sustain separations while simultaneously "resolving" antinomies.

According to the lady, both she and her maid will experience fullness, completion. The lady, bestowing upon her lover a mark of her own spirituality, expects to find her carnality complemented by an ethereal "sigh" emitted by "all the labouring heavens" in the course of their correspondent toil. Just as the lady's chaste kiss prompts a sound reminiscent of the tone of life after the Fall, so too the "fallen" chambermaid, tasting earthy fruit, evokes the harmonies of "Translunar Paradise."

As above, so below: that is not only the question here but a form of answer as well. On whatever level we choose to ponder it, Yeats's Hermetic formula operates throughout the closing lines. We recall, for example, Ribh's exposition of "an Older Theology":

> *Natural and supernatural with the self-same ring are wed.*
> *As man, as beast, as an ephemeral fly begets, Godhead*
>   *begets Godhead,*
> *For things below are copies, the Great Smaragdine*
>   *Tablet said.*[6]

When we scrutinize how "things" in this poem are complemented, we note also that "contrapuntal serpent hiss" is itself counterpointed by the sighing heavens. Like the "single root" of the ballad which begat these lyrics, the wonder of this poem lies in its beguiling tangle of variously combined elements, for both antinomy and "resolution" are implicit in the scheme *kiss:hiss:: thigh:sigh*. Indeed, awed by the fearful symmetry of the last four lines, we may with good reason say again, *"The Lord have mercy upon us."*

"Sighs" and "thighs" are the concern of the lover, a dreamy
romantic who in his own way demonstrates better than most of
Yeats's *personae* "The Thinking of the Body." Whereas for the
clever lady "consummation" is primarily a matter of rejecting
matter and having it too, for the lover, no crafty artificer, it is
something that comes most naturally:

> *Bird sighs for the air,*
> *Thought for I know not where,*
> *For the womb the seed sighs.*
> *Now sings the same rest*
> *On mind, on nest,*
> *On straining thighs.*

The shortest poem of the sequence, this lyric is also the most
breath-taking. Focusing on the mystery of sexual desire, Yeats
deftly explores the nature of ideality as he expresses both in
theme and form the stasis to which all desire should move.

Nature, a wedding of matter and spirit, provides appropriate
analogue for the perfection ("rest") achieved by the lover, who,
having sprung his seed, quietly becomes attuned to the unity of
all creation. As spiritual bird, an emblem also of wholeness, "sighs"
for its airy home, so too material seed, not yet quickened, "sighs"
for its release to the "womb," that nesting, resting place where
all matter becomes vital. Both bird and man are related by virtue
of this primal longing inherent in each: in the same instinctual
way that bird longs for the air, man, seeking to express his love,
would climb to his own proper place. (Or, to turn the figure,
would "descend/From emblematical niches" for "desecration and
the lover's night."[7]) Though his thought take flight and he dream
of higher, undefinable things, the lover nevertheless calmly accepts the "rest" that comes to mind and body alike. Though
ultimately his experience of the ideal is grounded in our world
of the "dying"[8] generations, what is important here is that passion's burden, pressing heavily on both body and soul, mind and
thigh, is discharged and resolved at last.

By nature and temperament two decidedly different people,
the lady and the lover are able nevertheless to attain a very satisfying resolution. "Consummation" for the lady, we have seen, is
mainly an intellectual affair, her "rest" that which follows the
imaginative exercise of mental gymnastics. For the lover, how-

ever, who does not even "know" where "thought" "sighs for," it is simply a question of making some simple connections (animal nature and humankind, body and soul, male and female) and being thankful for what comes. Perhaps it may be said of both "The Lady's Third Song" and "The Lover's Song" that the "consummation" central to each affords the speakers not merely an intensely satisfying experience but also one that could be called an "artifice of eternity." As with the concluding lines of the lady's closing song, here again poetic form not only establishes and heightens experience but, presenting it, comes to *be* that experience. Clearly, in both these poems Yeats has been able to communicate completeness by designing symbolic constructs of consummate artistry.

The shape of "The Lover's Song" may be plotted as a rising and falling movement characteristic of the course of love's energy. This pattern of desire, suspension, and rest is expressed in the *a a b c c b* rhyme scheme: after *a a* we get *b*, and expecting *b* again, we get instead suspense, *c*, doubled in the fifth line until resolution, *b*, is achieved at last. This resolution is foreshadowed by the satisfying shape of the first three lines, the sighing half of the poem, where a chiasmus ("sighs" on the ends, aspirated "*wh*ere" and the gliding semi-vowel of "*w*omb" in the middle) both heightens the lover's desire and anticipates his "straining" release. As for sound, we should note that sibilant consonants, recalling the "serpent hiss" of the previous poem and anticipating the deflated "worm" image of the next two, occur twelve times. Dominating the poem, these sibilants, along with the voiceless initial consonants (where the breath hisses through with a fricative sound) of opposing "thought" and "thighs," occur only in stressed syllables. Further, we are struck by the distinctive balance of the last two lines, the only ones composed regularly. Most striking perhaps is the final line, where "straining" (the only word of more than one syllable), straddling both iambic feet, symbolically holds the balance of the poem's theme as well as of the poem itself as it reminds us of "sexual spasm."

The last two songs of the sequence belong to the chambermaid, a realist who appropriately has the last word. "What's left to sigh for?" she asks as she brings us back to mundane reality. Earthy, her two songs present not only the intrusion of reality after an experience of the ideal but, questioning, draw us into questions of our own concerning the encounter face to face of persons sighing and straining for communion.

Thus the first song reveals man and woman not as "the yolk and white of the one shell,"[9] but as "stranger with stranger":

> *How came this ranger*
> *Now sunk in rest*
> *Stranger with stranger,*
> *On my cold breast?*
> *What's left to sigh for?*
> *Strange night has come;*
> *God's love has hidden him*
> *Out of all harm,*
> *Pleasure has made him*
> *Weak as a worm.*

Though the romantic lover has sought the warmth of a "nest" and the "rest" promised therein, the chambermaid, given to plain talk, describes this sighing wanderer as lost in the bare coldness of her breast. ("Now *sunk* in rest," an ironic echo of "Now *sinks* the same rest" of "The Lover's Song," is richly ambiguous: here denoting lapse from mental activity, the verb connotes "ruinous fall," "degeneration," as well as "happy relaxation," "rewarding descent.") His "pleasure," having neither shaken heaven nor elicited portentous serpent sounds, has left him instead "harmless." "Strange night," for the woman not the blissful oblivion anticipated by the dreaming young man, finds her very much awake, wondering about the "mystery" of the male and of the mysterious union just consummated. Her meditation, an analogue for the sex act before and after, works its way from lusty and commanding "ranger" ("a common Anglo-Irish term, expressing at once admiration, and virility, and a shadow of alarm"[10]) to detumescent and puny "worm." Clearly, romantic man, who would soar like a bird, labors under limitations. From beginning to end, from "ranger" to "worm," this is the pattern of all human experience, the knowing chambermaid suggests. Once again, both theme and form conspire not only to frame what is otherwise incommunicable but also to insinuate that esteemed man, self-deceived, is destined to "exhaust his glory and his might."

The pattern plotted from "ranger" to "worm" is not altogether pathetic. "Limp" man, weakened by "pleasure" yet possessing neither the chambermaid's nor the lady's love, nevertheless gains

the protective love of God. This situation, which may be analogous to that of Yeats in old age, seems to suggest here, and
throughout *Last Poems* as well, that as man exhausts human possibility, like Lear (an important mask for Yeats during his last
years) he discovers himself stripped to bare, elemental stuff.
Bereft of all "lendings" but hardened by passion, as naked essence
he makes love not to man or to woman but to "the void,"[11] a
cavelike enclosure which God provides for otherwise "unaccommodated man" to be "hidden . . . out of all harm."[12]

Thrice repeated "worm," dominating the imagery of "The
Chambermaid's Second Song" as well as controlling its syntax,
brings the sequence to a sobering close. "The summing up," Yeats
termed this lyric,[13] and well it is:

> *From pleasure of the bed,*
> *Dull as a worm,*
> *His rod and its butting head*
> *Limp as a worm,*
> *His spirit that has fled*
> *Blind as a worm.*[14]

Simpler in form and more limited in theme than the previous
poem, this concluding lyric reiterates and reinforces the "stranger
with stranger" motif of its companion piece. The "consummation," though physically accomplished, still leaves the man and
woman detached. The unity that figured so impressively and importantly in earlier poems of the sequence Yeats now shows to
have been a fiction. Sexual union, the chambermaid knows, is
only a temporary juncture, a pleasurable but very transitory
coming together. This theme of the lack of true fulfillment, the
fundamental incompleteness of the act, seems to be reflected in
the form of the poem, in the fact that it lacks the solidity of even
a single predicate.

To appreciate better the import of the chambermaid's two
songs and thus the entire sequence, it is well to recall John Spar-
row's account of a conversation with Yeats in 1931. Discussing
"the metaphysical antinomy of the individual and the infinite,
the many and the one," Yeats praised the description of sexual
intercourse in Dryden's translation of Lucretius because "it was
introduced to illustrate the difficulty of two becoming a unity:
'The tragedy of sexual intercourse is the perpetual virginity of

the soul.' Sexual intercourse is an attempt to solve the eternal antinomy, doomed to failure because it takes place on only one side of the gulf. The gulf is that which separates the one and the many, or if you like, God and man."[15]

With these ideas in mind we may now view "The Lady's Third Song" (for example) as even more momentous, for we see that the speaker, a skilled philosopher, not only resolves her dilemma but also proceeds to bridge the "gulf" which Yeats likened to the celebrated Parmenidean chasm. As far as she is concerned, we might suppose, "the eternal antinomy" has been resolved. From her point of view, both in the metaphysical as well as in the sexual sense, two, "participating" in one, have "become" one.

From the chambermaid's point of view, however, this resolution was merely fanciful, or at best only a fleeting thing.[16] By the end of the sequence, Yeats strongly suggests the tragic irresolution of "the eternal antinomy." The lover and the chambermaid were "doomed to failure" because of necessity their communion took place "on only one side of the gulf." Thus, the fact that the lover's partner is not really his beloved, a detail carrying over from the initial ballad, now gains in significance. It not only accentuates the lover's deception but boldly and unmistakably symbolizes as well the unromantic truth of human apartness. "Everywhere," Yeats said shortly before composing the sequence, we encounter "that antinomy of the One and the Many that Plato thought in his *Parmenides* insoluble, though Blake thought it soluble 'at the bottom of the graves.' "[17] Though this idea may not have motivated Yeats to write "The Three Bushes," surely it is the premise upon which the entire cycle of lyrics eventually turns.

Thus, to Vivienne Koch's question, "Why . . . with a pretty and almost 'poetical' ending to his opening ballad, does Yeats allow the little drama to trail off in the let-down cadences of the Chambermaid's second song?"[18] I would reply that in all the attendant lyrics the speaking voice emphasizes the existential reality, the separateness of the lovers, and that Yeats deliberately gave the last word to the chambermaid because her view most acutely emphasizes the impossibility of man's achieving his desired state of wholeness. (Again, it is well to remember that Yeats termed her second song "the summing up.") Only in ballads and in other artifacts are fabulous artifices more acceptable than the sober facts of life themselves. Only God may dwell in a world of pure essence; men and women must live as prisoners in private worlds of existence. It is the sober chambermaid, not the lettered lady or the yearning lover, who is most aware of the actual nature of this absurd human condition. She has lain amid foul rag and bone knowing that there if anywhere is where all ladders of ascension rise. She sings the last two songs because only two years earlier, in "A Prayer for Old Age," Yeats himself sang:

> God guard me from those thoughts men think
> In the mind alone;
> He that sings a lasting song
> Thinks in a marrow-bone.

Moreover, of the three *personae* in the sequence, she represents not the most desirable but the most fitting mask for the poet who in old age developed a profound sense of pathos for man's lonely and finite condition, and who, after more than forty years of glorious "sailing," finally forsook "fairyland" for the "real world" and thus came to terms with the fact of mortality that binds men together and ties them to the things of time.

In more than one sense, then, are the divisions which we have encountered—day and night, upper and lower, breast and limb, ranger and worm—important; for to these we may now add "the one and the many . . . God and man," and consequently must look upon the fancied union of body and soul as but another illustration of the "manifold illusion" by which, we read in "Meru," "Civilization is hooped together."

From this last perspective, surely an ultimate one, we discover further meaning in the obvious analogy between "serpent" and "worm." What these poems suggest ultimately, we realize now, is the tragic lot of fallen man. Not only as persons, as halves of a sundered whole, but as emblems also of divided worlds and dissociated sensibilities, man and woman must forever ache for wholeness. Because they bear the taint of mortality, our "consummations" are now imperfect and impermanent, Yeats suggests. But ever mindful of last things, he bids the "dying generations" look to "the Day of Judgment":

> "What can be shown?
> What true love be?
> All could be known or shown
> If Time were but gone."
> "That's certainly the case," said he.

CONCLUSION ✳ RECONCILIATION WITH TIME

COUNTERFEITS of eternity exist only chimerically. Symbolic structures, no matter how engaging, remain but analogies of experiences real or imagined. Though subtly ordered and charged with superior meaning, supreme fictions derive their existence from a mundane world abounding in living and dying things. Though art and artful resolutions may to the artistic sensibility seem more alive than life itself, Yeats in old age discovered what Axël and others of his tragic generation did not—that art is not life and our servants cannot live it for us.

In this study of the poetry of Yeats's old age I have tried to explore the relationship between existential awareness and artistic vitality. Convinced that during the final years of his life he finally came to terms with the inescapable burden of time, I began by plotting an opposing line of development, the "escape" motif, which Yeats was to abandon only after encountering the reality of very real death. Dominating his work from its very beginning, the theme of what he called "a flight into fairyland from the real world, and a summons to that flight," was countered, I contend, when, on the brink of the grave from 1927 on, Yeats came to affirm commitments and engagements from which in "the living world" there is no escape.

For all the marvel of his mounting mind, Yeats was not really interested in "philosophy" as our age commonly conceives it. Thus, never a "true believer," he was destined to make poems and to continue remaking himself amidst tortuous and never-ending vacillations. From the many modalities assumed by these vacillations there emerges a basic affirmation of "I am"—I am, and therefore I think, and therefore all else. Herein for Yeats lies the core of the much-craved and mysterious "last knowledge" that in 1917 he said "has often come most quickly to turbulent men"; and as he foresaw then, it was inevitable that "for a new season" it should bring "new turbulence." Forever frustrated in his early rage for essence, he came instead to lust for the fullness of existence. Never attaining the "one clear view" that he so desperately and persistently sought from the days of his adolescence, he nonetheless was able ultimately to wring meaning from despair, to apprehend modes of order amidst cycles of universal disorder. It is this final vision, at once consummate and consuming, that finally enabled him to bring the grand design of his "Sacred Book" to wholeness, that transformed his last season of silliness and turbulence into a thing of terrible beauty. Miguel de Unamuno, quick to sense the tragic grandeur of the Quixotic conscience, summed it all: "And may God deny you peace, but give you glory!"

Wholeness, then, is the condition to which Yeats finally wrought both his life and work and their intriguing tangle. The lyrics written beyond Byzantium show an old man who, reviewing old themes and passing new judgments, reached out in new directions. This coherent body of poems reveals a counterbalancing tendency, a vital compulsion to present and preserve what previously he had ignored or denounced. Much of its impressive power grows not only from the formal and ideational tensions implicit in the poems themselves, but also from our awareness of the import of these poems in the larger context of Yeats's total development. What is most significant about them, and why they bring his life's work to "wholeness," i.e., integrity, is that their otherness is complementary—"serving to fill out or complete." Though Yeats left many problems unsolved, was puzzled by new ones, and at best found only partial and tentative answers, during the last phase of his life he greatly enlarged his vision and broadened the base of his understanding, and in so doing he painfully came to derive more significant meaning from the experience of being human.

As we have seen, the winding "way of the chameleon" led Yeats to soul-satisfying Byzantium, and beyond Byzantium to existential ways demanded by the wholeness of his being. Body and soul in their oneness—the whole man—conspired to create a startling world starkly true to dramatic patterns of conflict and crisis. Whatever the mask he assumed, he remained an existential man of the West, a man of flesh and blood with Europe in his bones. A man of time, our time, he turned aside from unheroic postures presented by the uncomprehending East; and thus the hard lineaments of his chiseled last poems show a poet committed to rising above "All Asiatic vague immensities." The drama of the last years of Yeats's life may be seen as a kind of Marathon of our day: "Born into that ancient sect" that made tragic awareness possible, "But thrown upon this filthy modern tide," Yeats found his own "proper dark" and made it grow luminous. He fleshed it with concretions tender for their transience yet tough because they embody tensions made from the stuff of time.

Though "All" might be revealed "If Time were but gone," Yeats learned that tragic gaiety committed him to seeking freedom within the restricting limits of temporal possibility. His romanticism, now tempered by a true "vision of evil," pushed him into the mainstream of English poetry yet allowed him to gain perspectives denied to the more limited men from whom he early learned his craft. "Bitter and gay" lay the tragic scene beyond Byzantium, and it was there that he finally reached a reconciliation with "Time." Not transcendence, however, but the simple triumph of trying to be a total man was Yeats's final accomplishment. After all the anguish and the judgments, he repented nothing. Like Gide's Theseus, conqueror of a labyrinth and builder of a humane city, at the close of his life Yeats could honestly declare the only truth ultimately worth telling: "I have lived."

✻ ACKNOWLEDGEMENTS

Selections from W. B. Yeats's *Collected Poems* are reprinted with permission of The Macmillan Company, © 1903, 1906, 1907, 1912, 1916, 1918, 1919, 1924, 1928, 1931, 1933, 1934, 1935, 1940, 1944, 1945, 1946, 1950, 1956 by The Macmillan Company; © 1940 by Georgie Yeats; © renewed 1931, 1934, 1935 by William Butler Yeats; © renewed 1940, 1944, 1945, 1946, 1952 by Bertha Georgie Yeats; © renewed 1956 by Georgie Yeats; © renewed 1961, 1962 by Bertha Georgie Yeats; © renewed 1968 by Bertha Georgie Yeats, Michael Butler Yeats, and Anne Yeats. Selections from *Essays and Introductions* are reprinted with permission of The Macmillan Company, © 1961 by Mrs. W. B. Yeats; from *The Letters of W. B. Yeats*, ed. Alan Wade, reprinted with permission of The Macmillan Company, © 1953, 1954 by Anne Butler Yeats; from *A Vision*, reprinted with permission of The MacMillan Company, © 1937 by The Macmillan Company, renewed 1965 by Bertha Georgie Yeats and Anne Butler Yeats. Permission from A. P. Watt & Son, London, to use the various extracts from poems and prose works of W. B. Yeats is also gratefully acknowledged.

Yeats's Introduction to *The Oxford Book of Modern Verse* is quoted with permission of the Clarendon Press, Oxford. *Letters from W. B. Yeats to Dorothy Wellesley* is quoted with permission of the Oxford University Press.

Frank O'Connor's *Kings, Lords & Commons* is quoted with permission of Alfred A. Knopf; W. H. Auden's *Homage to Clio* with permission of Random House and Faber and Faber.

The substance of Chapter Seven was originally published in *Criticism* 7, Summer 1965, and appears here by permission of the Wayne State University Press. A portion of Chapter Six was originally published in *Arizona Quarterly* 21, Autumn 1965, and appears here by permission of its editors, as do two notes (embodied in Chapters Three and Five) published in *English Language Notes* 2, 1965.

❋ NOTES

Notes to Introduction

1. "Anima Hominis," *Mythologies* (London: Macmillan, 1959), p. 342.
2. The ancestral home of the Gore-Booth sisters; see "In Memory of Eva Gore-Booth and Con Markiewicz." In 1927 Lady Gregory sold Coole (house and park) to the Land Commission and Forestry Department and became a tenant. Soon after Yeats's death, the house, sold again, was pulled down.
3. Letter to H. J. C. Grierson, 14 November 1922. *The Letters of W. B. Yeats,* ed. Allan Wade (New York: Macmillan, 1955), p. 570. Hereafter cited as Wade.
4. Letter to Olivia Shakespear, 30 June 1932. *Ibid.,* p. 798.
5. Letter of 6 July 1935. *Letters on Poetry from W. B. Yeats to Dorothy Wellesley* (London: Oxford University Press, 1940), p. 9. Hereafter cited as *DW*.
6. See text of B.B.C. broadcast of 11 October 1936, *Essays and Introductions* (London: Macmillan, 1961), p. 502.

Notes to Chapter One

1. Letter of 30 June 1932. Wade, p. 798.
2. See *A Concordance to the Poems of W. B. Yeats,* ed. Stephen Maxfield Parrish (Ithaca: Cornell University Press, 1963).
3. The poem was printed in *The Wanderings of Oisin and Other*

Poems (1889) and was left out of all subsequent editions. For text see *The Variorum Edition of the Poems of W. B. Yeats*, ed. Peter Allt and Russell K. Alspach (New York: Macmillan, 1957), pp. 720-22.

4. Cf. the description of the old man in *At the Hawk's Well:* "He is all doubled up with age;/The old thorn-trees are doubled so/ Among the rocks where he is climbing."

5. See "The Coming of Wisdom with Time," written March 1909, and first published in 1910 under the title "Youth and Age."

6. In a later poem, "Why Should not Old Men be Mad?" Yeats refers to a similar change in Maud Gonne: "A Helen of social welfare dream,/Climb on a wagonette to scream." Joseph Hone remarks that "there seemed to be some physical resemblance between Constance Gore-Booth and Maud Gonne." *W. B. Yeats, 1865-1939* (London: Macmillan, 1942), pp. 115-16.

7. *Variorum*, pp. 750, 762. Later in the poem we find a related metaphor: ". . . young Aengus in his tower of glass,/Where time is drowned in odour-laden winds/And druid moons, and murmuring of boughs . . . ." (p. 762.)

8. "A Visionary," *Mythologies*, pp. 13-14. Yeats mentions the incident again in "The Trembling of the Veil": "Russell has just come in from a long walk on the Two Rock mountain, very full of his conversation with an old religious beggar, who kept repeating, 'God possesses the heavens, but He covets the earth.'" *Autobiographies* (London: Macmillan, 1955), p. 249. One is reminded of Blake's "Eternity is in love with the productions of time." *(The Marriage of Heaven and Hell)* Cf. also Aoife's cry in "The Grey Rock": "Why must the lasting love what passes?"

9. There may be an ironic echo of the Scriptural account (St. Matthew 17, St. Mark 9) of the Transfiguration of Jesus, where "his face did shine as the sun, and his raiment was white as the light," and where a voice from an overshadowing bright cloud cried, "This is my beloved Son."

10. In early editions of his poems Yeats glossed *fret* as "doom or destiny."

11. "The Trembling of the Veil," *Autobiographies*, pp. 115-16.

12. Ralph Waldo Emerson, "Ode to W. H. Channing."

13. Letter to Katharine Tynan, 6 February 1889. Wade, p. 111. Cf. "The Circus Animals' Desertion."

14. See *Variorum*, p. 717.

15. For a discussion of the revisions see Thomas Parkinson, *W. B. Yeats, Self-Critic* (Berkeley: University of California Press, 1951), pp. 39-46. Parkinson demonstrates that the poem "shows all the types of change made from 1889 to 1901 as in a microcosm; the removal of inversions, the change of archaism, the attempt to use specific language, the clearer sense of structural economy."

16. *Autobiographies*, p. 153.

17. *John Sherman and Dhoya* (London: Unwin, 1891), pp. 122-23. Published under the pseudonym "Ganconagh."

18. Letter of 21 December 1888. Wade, pp. 99-100.

19. She married a Boer War hero whom Yeats, while eulogizing him in "Easter, 1916," nevertheless termed "a drunken vain-glorious lout"—a description at least consistent with the remark he had imputed to Maud a few years earlier in the prize-winning "The Grey Rock": "In two or three years/I must needs marry some poor lout." "Ah yes," she says she wrote to Yeats, "you are happy without me, because you make beautiful poetry out of what you call your unhappiness and you are happy in that. Marriage would be such a dull affair. Poets should never marry. The world should thank me for not marrying you." Maud Gonne MacBride, *A Servant of the Queen* (London: Gollancz, 1938), p. 329.

20. A. Norman Jeffares, *W. B. Yeats, Man and Poet* (New Haven: Yale University Press, 1949), p. 68.

21. "To an Isle in the Water."

22. "The Heart of the Spring," *Mythologies*, pp. 173-74.

23. Letter to Katharine Tynan, 14 March 1888. Wade, p. 63.

24. Letter to Olivia Shakespear, 7 June 1922. Wade, p. 685. Mrs. Shakespear, the mysterious "Diana Vernon" of Yeats's early writings, was Lionel Johnson's cousin and Ezra Pound's mother-in-law. A close friend for thirty-eight years, she was Yeats's mistress during the mid-Nineties (see Yeats's account of the affair in an unpublished autobiographical fragment quoted in Jeffares, *W. B. Yeats, Man and Poet*, pp. 100-101), and it was to her that Yeats addressed his "After Long Silence" three years before her death in 1932 (see Wade, pp. 771-72).

25. Both Jon Stallworthy and Curtis Bradford have reconstructed the composition of the poem after collating numerous MSS. See Jon Stallworthy, *Between the Lines: W. B. Yeats's Poetry in the Making* (Oxford: Clarendon Press, 1963), pp. 87-112; and Curtis Bradford, "Yeats's Byzantium Poems: A Study of Their Development," in *Yeats: A Collection of Critical Essays*, ed. John Unterecker (Englewood Cliffs, N.J.: Prentice-Hall, 1963), pp. 93-100—a revised version of an article originally appearing in *PMLA* 75 (1960): 110-25. This fascinating study of the development of several plays, poems, and prose works, while helpfully sampling the full range of Yeats's literary art, is of necessity focused only briefly on material relevant to the last phase of his career. Bradford's subsequent critique of the order of arrangement of the last poems as printed in the Macmillan edition of *Last Poems and Plays* and preserved in the *Variorum* deserves to be followed up by a systematic and thorough study of the manuscript and publishing history of the last poems, and by a more reliable edition of these poems. See "Yeats's *Last Poems* Again," in *The Dolmen Press Yeats Centenary Papers*, ed. Liam Miller (Dublin: The Dolmen Press, 1968), pp. 257-88. Jon Stallworthy's *Vision and Revision in Yeats's "Last Poems"* (London: Oxford University Press, 1969)—which became available only after my study was at the printer's—represents a step in the needed direction.

26. A. Norman Jeffares notes that "in Celtic legendary the salmon

is used as a symbol of strength; the hero Cuchulain is renowned for his 'salmon leap.' " See "The Byzantine Poems of Yeats," *Review of English Studies* 22 (1946): 47.

27. Cf. "The Trembling of the Veil": "When I was a child and went daily to the sexton's daughter for writing lessons, I found one poem in her School Reader that delighted me beyond all others: a fragment of some metrical translation from Aristophanes wherein birds sing scorn upon mankind." (*Autobiographies*, p. 171.)

28. In "The Tables of the Law" Yeats declared that "the world only exists to be a tale in the ears of coming generations; and terror and content, birth and death, love and hatred, and the fruit of the Tree, are but instruments of that supreme art which is to win us from life and gather us into eternity like doves into their dove-cots." (*Mythologies*, pp. 300-301.)

Notes to Chapter Two

1. Quoted from *Webster's New International Dictionary*, 2d ed.

2. *The Literary Symbol* (New York: Columbia University Press, 1955), p. 249.

3. Yeats beguiles us not only with ambivalence but with other ambiguities as well. Witness "The Secret Rose": awaiting that potent flower's "great wind of love and hate," Yeats asks, "When shall the stars be blown about the sky,/Like the sparks blown out of a smithy, and die?"—and seeming to answer, ends by posing yet another question: "Surely thine hour has come, thy great wind blows,/Far off, most secret, and inviolate Rose?" In a related connection, Tindall, anatomizing ambiguities, observes: "The questions with which Yeats liked to end his poems are ambivalent. Seeming statements bringing assurance and resolving conflicts, they acquire uncertainty when questioned at the end. 'Among School Children' becomes less final than we thought before feeling its punctuation." (*The Literary Symbol*, p. 232.)

4. Letter to L. A. G. Strong, 4 December 1931. Wade, p. 788.

5. The exact date of "A Dialogue of Self and Soul" is uncertain. In a letter dated 2 (or 4) October 1927, Yeats announced that he was writing "a new tower poem 'Sword and Tower,' which is a choice of rebirth rather than deliverance from birth" (Wade, p. 729); but in a note appended to the published poem he said that it was "written in the spring of 1928 during a long illness." (Yeats suffered from congestion of the lungs in October 1927. Traveling south to Spain and France, he had an attack of influenza in January 1928, while in Cannes, and a month later journeyed to Rapallo to convalesce.) Jeffares mentions that the poem was begun after July 1927—*W. B. Yeats, Man and Poet*, p. 247; and Ellmann dates it July-December 1927—*The Identity of Yeats* (London: Macmillan, 1954), p. 291. If we can depend on Yeats's memory (the poem and note were first published in

1933), I would conjecture that part one was written before his physical collapse, and that his note properly refers only to the second part. This would explain the two-part structure of the poem and would perhaps account for the different approach evident in the striking second part.

6. Dated 2 (or 4) October 1927. Wade, p. 729.

7. Letter of 24 September (?1927). Wade, p. 728. There is an ironic echo of the Anglican Office for the Burial of the Dead: "In the midst of life we are in death."

8. See letter to Olivia Shakespear, 2 July 1929. Wade, p. 764.

9. Letter dated 17 August 1933. *Ibid.*, p. 814.

10. See the closing lines of *A Full Moon in March*.

11. Letter to Olivia Shakespear, 23 November 1931. Wade, pp. 785-86. See below, n. 43, for more on possible source.

12. Letter to Olivia Shakespear, 20 September 1933. *Ibid.*, p. 815.

13. Though the Bishop functions in the poem more as a symbol of cruelty and inhumanity than as a spokesman for clerical reaction, he is kin to "a Connaught Bishop" who "told his people . . . that they 'should never read stories about the degenerating passion of love.'" See *Plays and Controversies* (London: Macmillan, 1923), p. 53.

14. Unterecker, p. 226.

15. T. R. Henn, observing in the second stanza "the reduction of man to the bundle of rags, and love to the sexual act," sees the influence of Swift. Yeats, he suggests, "made Crazy Jane (as Swift had made Vanessa) to see that unaccommodated men or women must be stripped in just this way before wisdom can replace illusion." *The Lonely Tower* (London, Methuen, 1950), p. 41. Henn's suggestion seems all the more likely when we consider that around this time Yeats made frequent mention of Swift in his poems, letters, and essays, and that in 1930 he had written *The Words upon the Window Pane* and had translated Swift's epitaph.

16. *The Golden Nightingale* (New York: Macmillan, 1949), p. 158, n. 34.

17. *The Marriage of Heaven and Hell*. The third and fourth lines of the stanza recall Blake's *Jerusalem* (IV. 88): "For I will make their places of joy and love excrementitious."

18. Introduction to *An Indian Monk* (1932), in *Essays and Introductions*, p. 431. John Unterecker identifies the saint as Cruchan—*A Reader's Guide to William Butler Yeats* (New York: Noonday Press, 1959), p. 234. Yeats, however, in the passage cited above, says he has forgotten the name; expressing uncertainty ("Was it Columbanus or another?") he quotes virtually the same statement elsewhere—see "Discoveries" and the 1937 "A General Introduction for my Work," *Essays and Introductions*, pp. 291, 514. Jeffares (*W. B. Yeats, Man and Poet*, p. 335), on the authority of Mrs. Yeats, says Cellach; Yeats himself, in a context analogous to the one at hand, refers to "that blessed Cellach who sang upon his deathbed of bird and beast"—see Commentary on Supernatural Songs in *Variorum*, p. 837.

19. "Crazy Jane on God."

20. *Le Testament*, 882, 892, 902, 909.

21. *America*.

22. "The Voice of the Devil," *The Marriage of Heaven and Hell.*

23. "Ribh Denounces Patrick."

24. See "Ribh at the Tomb of Baile and Aillinn."

25. "Ribh Denounces Patrick." Originally entitled "Ribh Prefers an Older Theology."

26. "Ribh Considers Christian Love Insufficient."

27. "Discoveries," *Essays and Introductions*, p. 267.

28. See James Joyce, *A Portrait of the Artist as a Young Man* (New York: Modern Library, n.d.), pp. 248-52.

29. *Ibid.*, p. 255.

30. Delmore Schwartz sketches some of the problems involved in attempting to discern "Yeats in Himself"; see *The Permanence of Yeats, ed.* James Hall and Martin Steinmann (New York: Macmillan, 1950), pp. 318-20.

31. Unterecker, p. 215.

32. Letter dated 30 June 1932. Wade, p. 798. This is the same letter in which Yeats expressed astonishment at finding "denunciation of old age" to pervade his work from *The Wanderings of Oisin* on.

33. Sir Thomas Browne, *Religio Medici*, I. xxxiv.

34. "Nineteen Hundred and Nineteen."

35. Discussing Valéry's *Le cimitière marin*, Yeats writes that "after certain poignant stanzas and just when I am deeply moved he chills me" because "he rejoices that human life must pass. I was about to put his poem among my sacred books, but I cannot now, for I do not believe him. My imagination goes some years backward, and I remember a beautiful young girl singing at the edge of the sea in Normandy words and music of her own composition. She thought herself alone, stood barefooted between sea and sand; sang with lifted head of the civilizations that there had come and gone, ending every verse with the cry: 'O Lord, let something remain.' " *A Vision* (New York: Macmillan, 1938), pp. 219-20. Yeats's note to this passage is worth recalling: he calls F. H. Bradley "an arrogant, sapless man" because that famed philosopher "hated the common heart."

36. This line originally read, "Can there be living speech in heaven's blue?" (Wade, p. 790.) In this letter to Olivia Shakespear (3 January 1932) Yeats says, "I shall be a sinful man to the end, and think upon my death-bed of all the nights I wasted in my youth."

37. Frank O'Connor writes: " 'I showed Lady Gregory a few weeks before her death a book by Day Lewis,' says Yeats. 'I prefer,' she said, 'those poems translated from the Irish, because they came out of original sin.' She prefers original sin because it is original and therefore not corrupted by thought. Yeats takes up the idea in a poem, *What theme had Homer but original sin?*" "Synge," in *The Irish Theatre*, ed. Lennox Robinson (London: Macmillan, 1939), p. 38. O'Connor may be quoting from Yeats's preface (p. xiv) to *The Ox-*

ford Book of Modern Verse (Oxford: Clarendon Press, 1936). Yeats, however, writes "by Frank O'Connor," not "from the Irish."

38. See Judges 14:5-18.

39. "In Memory of Major Robert Gregory."

40. Henn, *The Lonely Tower*, p. 75.

41. *A Vision*, p. 167.

42. See above, n. 20.

43. *The Lonely Tower*, p. 83. Jeffares (*W. B. Yeats, Man and Poet*, p. 333, n. 11A), commenting on Jane's genesis, suggests Synge's translation of Villon's "An Old Woman's Lamentations" as a possible source. (Villon's poem is entitled "*Les regrets de la belle Heaulmiere*" or "*La Vieille en regrettant le temps de sa jeunesse*"; see *Le Testament*, 453-532. Synge's translation is reprinted below Jeffares's note; Henn, presenting excerpts, suggests affinities with "Those Dancing Days are Gone" and other poems (*The Lonely Tower*, pp. 83-84).

44. *The Lonely Tower*, p. 73, n. 2.

45. "Discoveries," *Essays and Introductions*, pp. 277-78.

46. *A Vision*, p. 290.

47. "J. M. Synge and the Ireland of his Time," *Essays and Introductions*, p. 335.

48. All quoted material from here to the end of the paragraph is from "The Trembling of the Veil," *Autobiographies*, p. 273-74.

49. Dated 17 June 1935. *DW*, p. 6.

50. Dated 28 November 1935. *Ibid.*, pp. 43-44.

51. B.B.C. broadcast of 11 October 1936 ("Modern Poetry"). Quoted from text in *Essays and Introductions*, pp. 491-92. Cf. "The Trembling of the Veil," *Autobiographies*, p. 188.

52. Dated 24 June 1935. Wade, p. 836.

53. July 1936. *DW*, pp. 81-82.

NOTES TO CHAPTER THREE

1. Letter postmarked 9 February 1931. Wade, p. 781. Myths are "statements our nature is compelled to make and employ as a truth though there cannot be sufficient evidence." See Introduction to *The Resurrection*, in *Explorations* (London: Macmillan, 1962), p. 392.

2. Letter to Ethel Mannin, 20 October 1938. Wade, p. 918.

3. *Pages from a Diary Written in Nineteen Hundred and Thirty*, in *Explorations*, p. 290.

4. *A Vision*, p. 25.

5. "I feel . . . an unreality in French neo-Thomist movements, in T. S. Eliot's revival of seventeenth century divines." *Pages from a Diary Written in Nineteen Hundred and Thirty*, in *Explorations*, p. 334.

6. *A Vision*, pp. 270-71.

7. The songs were written in 1927, except for the last stanza, which

was first published in 1931. (Ellmann, *The Identity of Yeats*, p. 260.) Begun in 1925, the play was produced at the Abbey in 1934.

8. Commenting on these lines in his Introduction to *The Resurrection* (*Explorations*, p. 399), Yeats says that a "sense of spiritual reality comes whether to the individual or to crowds from some violent shock, and that idea has the support of tradition."

9. Letter dated 6 July 1935. *DW*, p. 8.

10. Letter received 1 January 1937. *Ibid.*, p. 128.

11. See "Ego Dominus Tuus."

12. Henn, *The Lonely Tower*, p. 303. Virginia Moore writes: "I suspect him of being Blake's Urizen, long sunk in abstract reason, a 'stony sleep' among the rocks, 'in chains of the mind locked up.'" *The Unicorn* (New York: Macmillan, 1954), p. 420. Ellmann, following a suggestion by Henn, notes that the Delphic Oracle "spoke through a cleft in the rock, and is a proper muse for a prophetic poem." *The Identity of Yeats*, p. 154. (In "The Man and the Echo" a "Rocky Voice" booms from "a cleft that's christened Alt." Though probably not intended to be taken seriously, John Unterecker's suggestion (*A Reader's Guide to William Butler Yeats*, p. 257) that "it might be the Rocky Face of the moon which controls the gyres and which peers from the cavern of night, so that theory had best be tacked on, too" nevertheless deserves mention.

13. See *W. B. Yeats, Man and Poet*, p. 289, and "Yeats' 'The Gyres': Sources and Symbolism," *Huntington Library Quarterly* 15 (1951): 90-93. Vivienne Koch's hysterical attack on Jeffares in *W. B. Yeats, The Tragic Phase* (London: Routledge and Kegan Paul, 1950)—see esp. pp. 94-95—is unwarranted, even though his statement in his biography that "Old Rocky Face is Shelley's Jew" suffers from injudicious use of the copula. One questions Miss Koch's assertion that "this frivolous importation adds nothing to the poem," but sympathizes with the substance of her argument that "even should the critic locate the right source for a particular symbol, he still hasn't told us why *it*, rather than some other detail of the poet's experience, was incorporated into the special affective complex which the poem is." (Jeffares's subsequent *HLQ* article does much to remove grounds for complaint.)

14. Curtis Bradford's redaction shows "Old Cavern man, old rocky face" side by side in an early draft. See *Yeats at Work* (Carbondale: Southern Illinois University Press, 1965), p. 145.

15. *Hellas*, 138-40, 146-48. The last lines, of course, recall the ending of "Sailing to Byzantium."

16. *Autobiographies*, p. 171.

17. *Ibid.*, p. 172. (*Hellas*, 152-54.)

18. *Hellas*, 746-47.

19. See *Hellas*, 1072-77, and "Two Songs from a Play."

20. Virgil, *The Pastoral Poems*, trans. E. V. Rieu (London: Penguin, 1949), p. 42.

21. Bradford, *Yeats at Work*, pp. 142-43.

22. Quoted in Henn, *The Lonely Tower*, p. 303.

23. *Hellas*, 197-98.

24. *Pages from a Diary Written in Nineteen Hundred and Thirty*, in *Explorations*, p. 296. See also Introduction to *Fighting the Waves* (*ibid.*, p. 375).

25. *Hellas*, 845-46.

26. Letter of 3 January 1932. Wade, p. 790. A draft of the seventh section of "Vacillation" is included in this letter. Cf. letter of 2 February 1928 to Sturge Moore, in *W. B. Yeats and T. Sturge Moore: Their Correspondence, 1901-1937*, ed. Ursula Bridge (New York: Oxford University Press, 1953), p. 122.

27. *The Literary Symbol*, pp. 207-8. Not sharing Yeats's double vision, George Brandon Saul unfortunately fails to find "justification for this somewhat revolting bit." *Prolegomena to the Study of Yeats's Poems* (Philadelphia: University of Pennsylvania Press, 1957), p. 137.

28. *The Lonely Tower*, p. 306. The owl, Athena's attendant and a familiar figure in the Parthenon, seems even more fitting when we consider that it is the only bird able to look straight forward, and that the cry to "look forth" (i.e., "observe what the gyres are doing" and "look to the future") in the first line controls much of the subsequent development of the poem.

29. *W. B. Yeats: The Tragic Phase*, p. 107.

30. *Polecat* < ME *polcat* < OF *pole, poule* (fowl) + *cat*.

31. I think it is necessary to regard "Or any rich, dark nothing" as dependent upon the previous phrase. Accordingly, I read it as elliptical for "any *such* rich, dark nothing," i.e., "of the type described by 'dark betwixt the polecat and the owl.'" Miss Koch's quotation from the stanza suggests that some of her difficulty stems from failure to scrutinize the adjective "any."

32. "*Primary* means democratic. *Antithetical* means aristocratic." *A Vision*, p. 104.

33. See the closing lines of "The Statues."

34. See pp. 67-68. The hoot of an owl in Yeats's garden at Oxford prompted one of these supernatural "communicators" to say, "Sounds like these . . . give us great pleasure" (p. 14).

35. *Pages from a Diary Written in Nineteen Hundred and Thirty*, in *Explorations*, p. 336.

36. "Anima Hominis," *Mythologies*, p. 332.

NOTES TO CHAPTER FOUR

1. "Hound Voice."

2. B.B.C. broadcast of 11 October 1936. Text in *Essays and Introductions*, p. 502.

3. According to Mrs. Yeats, the apparitions (actually seven in number) were "a series of death-dreams . . . of special significance in

relation to Lady Gregory's death, and to his own." Henn, *The Lonely Tower*, p. 140.

4. Yeats finished the poem ("almost the best I have made of recent years") on 25 July 1936, scarcely two months after his return from Spain. See letter of 26 July 1936, *DW*, p. 91.

5. "The Tragic Theatre" (1910), *Essays and Introductions*, p. 239.

6. "Anima Hominis," *Mythologies*, p. 332.

7. *DW*, pp. 8-9. Dated 6 July 1935.

8. "Under Ben Bulben," iii.

9. "Anima Hominis," *Mythologies*, p. 331.

10. The tone of the first stanza and the imagery of its concluding lines are inspired by the opening stanza of "The Boyne Water," a ballad included by Yeats and F. R. Higgins in their May 1935 issue of *Broadsides* (Dublin: Cuala Press) "because of its wildly picturesque description of that Williamite battle"—to quote from the headnote. The ballad (sometimes called "The Battle of the Boyne") begins: "July the first, of a morning clear, one thousand six hundred and ninety,/King James he pitched his tents between the lines for to retire/But King William threw his bomb balls and set them all on fire." A. Norman Jeffares, apparently unaware of the ballad's inclusion in *Broadsides*, nevertheless finds the same source: he observes that H. Halliday Sparling's 1888 edition of *Irish Minstrelsy*, an inscribed copy of which is in Yeats's library, includes the ballad. See Jeffares's "Notes on Yeats's 'Lapis Lazuli,' " *Modern Language Notes* 65 (1950): 489.

11. Henn (*The Lonely Tower*, p. xv) says that Yeats himself was "terrified" by the World War I Zeppelin raids.

12. "Poetry and Tradition" (1907), *Essays and Introductions*, p. 254.

13. "A General Introduction for my Work," *ibid.*, pp. 522-23. Dated 1937.

14. "Two Friends: Yeats and AE," *Yale Review* 29 (1939): 84-85. Quoting John O'Leary, Yeats writes in "The Trembling of the Veil": " 'There are things a man must not do to save a nation,' he had once told me, and when I asked what things, had said, 'To cry in public.' . . ." See *Autobiographies*, p. 213.

15. Letter to Olivia Shakespear, 29 November 1927. Wade, p. 733.

16. Dated 5 August 1936. *DW*, p. 94.

17. *King Lear*, II. ii. For association of tomb, womb, and *hysterica passio*, see "A Bronze Head." See "Parnell's Funeral" for correspondence between *hysterica passio* and "popular rage."

18. *Autobiographies*, p. 326.

19. Introduction, *The Oxford Book of Modern Verse*, p. xxxiv. The introduction is dated September 1936. A year later Yeats attributed the main idea to Lady Gregory, who rejected for Abbey production a play written "in the modern manner" because (in her words) "Tragedy must be a joy to the man who dies." (*Essays and Introductions*, p. 523.) In his last prose work Yeats wrote: "The arts are all the bridal chambers of joy. No tragedy is legitimate unless it

leads some great character to his final joy. Polonius may go out wretchedly, but I can hear the dance music in 'Absent thee from felicity awhile,' or in Hamlet's speech over the dead Ophelia, and what of Cleopatra's last farewells, Lear's rage under the lightning? . . . I add that 'will or energy is eternal delight,' and when its limit is reached it may become a pure, aimless joy. . . ." *On the Boiler*, in *Explorations*, pp. 448-49.

20. Cf. "The Three Hermits"; the third hermit, "Giddy with his hundredth year,/Sang unnoticed like a bird."

21. Introduction to *The Resurrection*, in *Explorations*, p. 396. More commonly termed *yin* and *yang* (Chinese *t'ai ch'ih*, "universality"), these are the cosmological principles of Tsao Yen (Third Century B.C.). In 1897 Yeats glossed the "pale deer" of an early poem as a symbol of "night and shadow," and in 1907 he observed that the speculations of Celtic scholars had made the "Death-pale Deer" and "The Boar without Bristles" "symbols of the end of all things." See *Variorum*, pp. 171, 843.

22. Cf. his statement in "Symbolism and Painting" (1898): "Only imperfection in a mirror of perfection, or perfection in a mirror of imperfection, delights our frailty." *Essays and Introductions*, p. 150.

23. *A Reader's Guide to William Butler Yeats*, p. 260. "Each accident of the stone," Unterecker adds, " 'seems' to have meaning, but that meaning—Yeats insists—is in the observer. . . . 'Meaning' hinges finally on the interplay that takes place between artist and art object, and between art object and audience."

24. "A Dialogue of Self and Soul."

25. See Jon Stallworthy, *Between the Lines*, p. 221.

NOTES TO CHAPTER FIVE

1. *The Unicorn from the Stars* (1907), *The Hour Glass* (1913). The former, based on *Where There is Nothing*, a 1902 play, goes back for idea to a story first published in 1896.

2. Letter to Edith Shackleton Heald, 21 February 1938. Wade, p. 906.

3. See "Ribh at the Tomb of Baile and Aillinn." Ellmann notes that Yeats was called "the eagle" by members of his family. (*The Identity of Yeats*, p. 209.)

4. Cf. Yeats's dream, *Autobiographies*, p. 283.

5. Unterecker, *A Reader's Guide to William Butler Yeats*, p. 289.

6. Letter of 9 October 1938. Wade, p. 917.

7. The first two lines quoted here are a later addition. For an earlier draft of the poem (July 1938), see *DW*, pp. 198-99.

8. From "Ballet, Pantomime and Poetic Drama" (1898). Quoted in Frank Kermode, *Romantic Image* (New York: Macmillan, 1957), p. 73.

9. *Ibid.*

10. Margot Ruddock (pseud. Margot Collis) was a young actress and aspiring poetess who, having once been told by Yeats to stop writing because her technique was deteriorating, visited Yeats unexpectedly in Majorca early one morning in May 1936. "I was amazed by the tragic magnificence of some fragments and said so," Yeats told Olivia Shakespear, and described how "she went out in pouring rain" in order to kill herself because then "her verse would live instead of her." See letter of 22 May 1936 (Wade, p. 856) for additional details of the episode.

11. Unterecker (*A Reader's Guide to William Butler Yeats*, p. 271) writes: "A serious parody, Yeats's gyrating drunkard moves in the elemental circles of that dance which brings sober vision to a dead drunk world."

12. See "The Double Vision of Michael Robartes."

13. *DW*, p. 8.

14. Wade, p. 867.

15. *DW*, pp. 127–28. Letter received 1 January 1937. On 21 December he had written (*DW*, p. 124): "I had a black fortnight the result of nervous strain writing the Casement poem. . . ."

16. *Ibid.*, p. 128

17. Letter of 28 November 1936. *Ibid.*, p. 117. Michael Yeats identifies the tune as that of "The Glen of Aherlow." See "W. B. Yeats and Irish Folk Song," *Southern Folklore Quarterly* 31 (1966): 173-74.

18. Hone, *W. B. Yeats, 1865–1939*, p. 450, n. 1. "Gone was the 'smiling public man,'" he says (p. 449), "in his place the rapparee from the Bog of Allen."

19. See Letter of 30 November 1936 to Ethel Mannin. Wade, p. 869.

20. DW, p. 117.

21. *Philadelphia Public Ledger*, 31 August 1916. Quoted in William J. Maloney, *The Forged Casement Diaries* (Dublin: Talbot Press, 1936), p. 105 and *passim*. Noyes, who wrote ineffectual, innocuously worded poems, gave no quarter when it came to criticism: "cess-pool," "poison," "decay," "entire contents of the garbage can," "attracting attention by pulling the lavatory chain," "filth," "dung-heap," he said of *Ulysses*, "introduced into England by a traitor now in a lunatic asylum." See *Two Worlds for Memory* (London: Sheed and Ward, 1953), pp. 218, 220-22.

22. By quoting from the *Philadelphia Public Ledger* article five times and erroneously suggesting that Noyes had spread similar propaganda in his other writings and speeches (Noyes delivered over two hundred public lectures while in this country), Maloney unfairly magnifies Noyes's role in blackening Casement's name. For the text of Noyes's disclaimer to the *Irish Press*, see his *Two Worlds for Memory*, pp. 126-30. Noyes later confessed in a letter to the *Times* (London) (17 May 1956) that the typewritten copy of the diaries *"was left with me for a few minutes* and was then somewhat hastily withdrawn." In *The Accusing Ghost of Roger Casement* (London: Gollancz, 1957) he argued that the diaries were forged. Nevertheless,

as a reviewer of this book properly asked, "And even if he did believe the forged documents to be genuine, on what standards of journalistic ethics did he permit himself to use this fact against a man whose supposed crime was treason?" (D. R., *Irish Independent*, 4 May 1957.)

23. For the text of Yeats's letter, see Wade, pp. 882-83.

24. *DW*, p. 119.

25. *Ibid.*, pp. 119-20.

26. *Ibid.*, p. 120.

27. *A Reader's Guide to William Butler Yeats*, pp. 269-70.

28. *DW*, pp. 121, 122.

29. On 10 December (*DW*, p. 122) Yeats told Dorothy Wellesley that he sent a "corrected Casement poem" to someone "very sad at having to cut out _____'s name." In all, the evidence points to a version of "Roger Casement" earlier than the one appearing in the *Irish Press* on 2 February 1937.

30. *DW*, p. 119.

31. Letter of 4 December 1936. *Ibid.*, p. 120.

32. "Academic Graffiti," in *Homage to Clio* (New York: Random House, 1960), p. 90.

33. Ezra Pound's comment on the "emotional" motif common to Shakespeare's *Timon of Athens* and Wyndham Lewis's "Timon" series. See *Gaudier-Brzeska, A Memoir* (London: John Lane, 1916), p. 107.

34. "Blood and the Moon," ii; letters to Lady Gregory (7 April 1930) and P. Wyndham Lewis (September 1930). Wade, pp. 773, 776.

35. *On the Boiler*, in *Explorations*, p. 435.

36. Letter of 23 December 1936. *DW*, p. 126.

37. Dated 21 January 1939. He died on the 28th. "After the Battle of Sligo in A.D. 537, Eoghan Bel 'was buried standing, his red javelin in his hand, as if bidding defiance to his enemies.'" (Henn, *The Lonely Tower*, p. 1.) Cf. Lord Raglan's *The Hero* (New York: Vintage Books, 1956), pp. 39-43 for the widespread myth of the Sleeping Warriors.

38. Letter of 30 November 1936. Wade, p. 869.

39. Letter of 11 December 1936. *Ibid.*, p. 873.

40. See "Under Ben Bulben" and *On the Boiler*.

41. R. A. Scott-James, "Editorial Notes," *London Mercury* 39 (1939): 479.

42. From Yeats's description of "John Kinsella's Lament for Mrs. Mary Moore." Letter to Edith Shackleton Heald, 21 July 1938. Wade, p. 912.

43. Henn, *The Lonely Tower*, p. 2.

44. Letter of 6 July 1935. *DW*, p. 9.

45. Letter postmarked 28 January 1937. *DW*, p. 135.

46. G. B. Saul notes that the second line of this stanza alludes to the Spartan boy mentioned in Plutarch's life of Lycurgus who "concealed a fox beneath his tunic and stoically ignored the vicious clawing and biting." *Prolegomena to the Study of Yeats's Poems*, p. 164.

For material elucidating the paradox "that things both can and cannot be," and the "great house" passage in the final stanza, see Bk. III of *A Vision* and the essay "Anima Hominis" (especially section eight). Cf. also "Crazy Jane on God" and *Purgatory.*

47. Letter of 8 January 1937. *DW*, p. 131.

48. T. R. Henn, "The Accent of Yeats' 'Last Poems,'" *Essays and Studies, 1956* (London: John Murray, 1956), p. 71, n. 1. Cf. Chap. Two, n. 15.

49. Letter of 8 January 1937. *DW*, p. 131.

50. "A General Introduction for my Work" (1937), *Essays and Introductions*, p. 516.

51. Letter of 5 September 1937. *DW*, p. 159.

52. Letter postmarked 28 January 1937. *Ibid.*, p. 135. In his *Southern Folklore Quarterly* article (175-76), Michael Yeats identifies the tune as that of "An Smachdaoin Crón," a Gaelic folk air that Yeats later replaced with an original one by Edmund Dulac "apparently performed once at least" but now lost.

53. See Higgins's essay, "Yeats as Irish Poet," in *Scattering Branches,* ed. Stephen Gwynn (New York: Macmillan, 1940), pp. 147-55.

54. Introduction to *The Oxford Book of Modern Verse*, pp. xiii-xiv.

55. William York Tindall, review of Frank O'Connor's *Kings, Lords & Commons* (New York: Knopf, 1959), *New York Herald Tribune Book Review*, 2 August 1959, p. 5. (O'Connor's book hereafter cited as *KLC.*) As for Yeats's enthusiasm, he included seven of O'Connor's translations in his *Oxford Book of Modern Verse;* only eight of the ninety-nine poets represented were allotted more poems.

56. Richard Ellmann has reproduced the MS copy of some of these poems along with the corrections suggested by Yeats. See *The Identity of Yeats*, pp. 194-200. With respect to the "bolder tone" which Yeats came to adopt after the turn of the century and which, as the evidence of the corrections suggests, he urged upon O'Connor, Ellmann quotes Yeats as saying to O'Connor: "You must always write as if you were shouting to a man across the street who you were afraid couldn't hear you, and trying to make him understand." (Conversation with O'Connor, *ibid.*, p. 201.)

57. Preface to *KLC*, p. v. See also Tindall's *Forces in Modern British Literature, 1885-1956* (New York: Vintage Books, 1956), pp. 78-79. With the first edition of this book (1946) Tindall was the first to suggest the "influence" of these translations. "Them" in O'Connor's statement refers to two earlier editions of translations, *The Wild Bird's Nest* (Dublin: Cuala Press, 1932), and *Lords and Commons* (Dublin: Cuala Press, 1938).

58. O'Connor's headnote to "Last Lines," *KLC*, p. 107.

59. "Last Lines," *ibid.*

60. "A Grey Eye Weeping," *ibid.*, p. 102. O'Connor recalls that the last line (repeated after each stanza) "caused us much anguish" because Yeats wanted "Has made me travel to seek you, Valentine Brown." " 'No beggars, no beggars!' he snapped irritably." "The Old

Age of a Poet," *The Bell* 1 (1941): 14. Yeats's line, certainly no improvement, was used when the poem was published in *The Wild Bird's Nest*, but not in the later *The Fountain of Magic* (London: Macmillan, 1939).

61. "The End of Clonmacnois," *KLC*, p. 46. "Whence are you, learning's son?"/"From Clonmacnois I come/My course of studies done,/I'm off to Swords again."/"How are things keeping there?"/ "Oh, things are shaping fair—/Foxes round the churchyards bare/ Gnawing the guts of men."

62. O'Connor's headnote, *ibid.*, p. 100.

63. *Ibid.*, p. 100. Cf. stanzas 4-6 of "The Municipal Gallery Revisited," discussed in Chap. Six. Cf. also Chap. Six, n. 21. Yeats must have realized that there was a point for point correspondence—sometimes literally, sometimes allegorically—between the material in these stanzas and what was true of Coole.

64. O'Connor's headnote, *ibid.*, p. 49.

65. *Ibid.*, pp. 34, 36, 60, 61. O'Connor describes the first figure as one who "returns to a land where because of the Christian monks everything has shrunk, grown cheap and ugly and old." Preface to *The Fountain of Magic*, p. viii.

66. Tindall's review of *KLC*. Cf. Yeats's comment on Jeremiah J. Callanan (1795-1829): "An honest style did not come into English-speaking Ireland until Callanan wrote three or four naive translations from the Gaelic." *A Book of Irish Verse*, ed. W. B. Yeats (London: Methuen, 1900), p. xix.

67. "Storm at Sea," *KLC*, p. 22. What O'Connor accepted and rejected here of Yeats's suggestions merits review. Originally (in MS) the second line quoted above began with "Bursts its frontiers," but Yeats suggested "Breaks down its barriers," and it is in this form that the line was published in *Lords and Commons* and *The Fountain of Magic*. O'Connor's compromise in *KLC* seems most fortunate. Further, the last line of this stanza, originally "Winter with his shining spear," was changed once and for all to the sharper, more active "Winter throws a shining spear," as Yeats suggested. Also, although Yeats offered revisions for O'Connor's competent original final stanza, he suggested that the entire stanza (which introduces religious references) be deleted. Apparently heeding Yeats's advice, O'Connor left the stanza out for the first two printings, but composed an even more "Christian" version when he restored the final stanza in *KLC*. (MS: "O God who broods above the swell,/The storm and all its fears repel,/Righteous captain of the feast,/Save us from the killing blast/ And guard us from tempestuous hell." *KLC*: "God's Son of hosts that none can tell/The fury of the storm repel!/Dread Lord of the sacrament,/Save me from the wind's intent,/Spare me from the blast of Hell.")

NOTES TO CHAPTER SIX

1. The reader of Peter Singleton-Gates and Maurice Girodias's *The Black Diaries of Roger Casement* (New York: Grove Press, 1959) is struck by the ironical antithesis all the more as he sees Casement's official reports on the left hand pages and his alleged secret writings on the right.

2. Quoted in Hone, *W. B. Yeats, 1865-1939*, p. 161.

3. Letter of 8 March 1909. Wade, p. 525. Cf. "On those that Hated 'The Playboy of the Western World,' 1907."

4. Letter to Lady Gregory, 2 January 1904. *Ibid.*, p. 422.

5. Hone, *W. B. Yeats, 1865-1939*, p. 344.

6. *Ibid.*

7. *Variorum*, p. 831.

8. See Hone, *W. B. Yeats, 1865-1939*, p. 382, and Hone's essay, "Yeats as Political Philosopher," *London Mercury* 39 (1939): 494.

9. See Frank O'Connor's autobiography, *An Only Child* (New York: Knopf, 1961), pp. 213-14, 237.

10. Dorothy Macardle, *The Irish Republic* (Dublin: Irish Press, 1951), p. 814. AE, for one, tried to save Childers. See *Lady Gregory's Journals, 1916-1930*, ed. Lennox Robinson (London: Putnam, 1946), p. 184. O'Connor, who knew Childers well, writes (*An Only Child*, pp. 237-38): "Again and again in my own imagination, I have had to go through those last few moments with him almost as though I were there: see the slight figure of the little grey-haired Englishman emerge for the last time into the Irish daylight, apparently cheerful and confident but incapable of grandiose gestures, concerned only lest inadvertently he might do or say something that would distress some poor fool of an Irish boy who was about to level an English rifle at his heart."

11. Edgar Holt, *Protest in Arms* (London: Putnam, 1960), p. 305. "The worse step yet," Lady Gregory called these reprisals. (*Journals*, p. 185.)

12. "What we were bringing about," O'Connor (*An Only Child*, p. 210) says of the Civil War, "was a new Establishment of Church and State in which imagination would play no part, and young men and women would emigrate to the ends of the earth, not because the country was poor, but because it was mediocre."

13. See Macardle, *The Irish Republic*, p. 47.

14. Griffith (1872-1922) is said to have died from "sheer exhaustion." (Hone, *W. B. Yeats, 1865-1939*, p. 349.)

15. Charles Ricketts, quoted in *ibid.*, pp. 225-26.

16. See "To a Wealthy Man Who Promised a Second Subscription to the Dublin Municipal Gallery if it were Proved the People Wanted Pictures."

17. *Lady Gregory's Journals*, p. 286. Robinson adds: "There are two portraits of Lane in our Municipal Gallery, one by Mancini showing him sitting on a sofa, febrile with exciting background, the Lane

that was the friend of Royalty and of the Peerage, the flashy Lane. The other is the Sargent portrait, the 'dreamer of dreams.'"

18. "Discoveries," *Essays and Introductions*, p. 278.

19. "The Bounty of Sweden," *Autobiographies*, pp. 553-54. At the very beginning of the fourth stanza Yeats immediately links Lady Gregory and Synge by means of the latter's comment on Mancini's portrait of her.

20. At Coole, Yeats says in "Coole Park, 1929," Synge and others "found pride established in humility." Oliver St. John Gogarty observes: "Lady Gregory . . . demanded either servility or respectability from all her acquaintances. Neither Joyce nor I had pliant knees." *William Butler Yeats: A Memoir* (Dublin: Dolmen Press, 1963), p. 9.

21. "In later years he was the born servant, even though it was of a phantom court . . . the Roman prelate, the secretary, the go-between; adept in courtesies and ready to serve any great man." Frank O'Connor, "The Old Age of a Poet," *The Bell* 1 (1941): 17-18. Cf. O'Connor's translation of "Kilcash," and above, Chap. Five, n. 63.

22. "Edmund Spenser," *Essays and Introductions*, pp. 359-60.

23. "The Poetry of W. B. Yeats," *Twentieth Century Literature* 6 (1960): 18.

24. *Variorum*, p. 839. At this affair Yeats made public a gift of money presented to him by a group of Americans. After the banquet, "The Municipal Gallery Revisited" was privately printed for presentation to those who had honored him.

25. *Ibid.*, pp. 839-40.

26. Yeats is referring to a speech made by his father during a public debate on *The Playboy of the Western World* held at the Abbey in January 1907. The elder Yeats recalls his words somewhat differently: "Of course I know Ireland is an island of Saints, but thank God it is also an island of sinners—only unfortunately in this Country people cannot live or die except behind a curtain of deceit." Letter of 29 December 1915 to Joseph Hone. J. B. Yeats, *Letters to His Son W. B. Yeats and Others, 1869-1922*, ed. Joseph Hone (London: Faber and Faber, 1944), p. 214.

27. "The Circus Animals' Desertion." *Engross*, denoting "take hold of completely," also connotes "enlarge."

28. James Joyce, *Stephen Hero*, ed. Theodore Spencer (Norfolk, Conn.: New Directions, 1944), p. 212.

29. See unpublished Yeats MS in Richard Ellmann, *The Identity of Yeats*, pp. 86-88. Also, *Finnegans Wake*, Chap. II, and Gogarty, *W. B. Yeats: A Memoir*, p. 10.

30. *Autobiographies*, p. 424.

31. *Ibid.*, p. 219.

32. *Ibid.*, p. 425.

33. So designated because he was the senior living member of a family in direct descent from the chieftain of a clan. One of the founders of the Irish Volunteers in 1913, he succeeded Casement as treasurer.

34. Holt, *Protest in Arms*, p. 98.

35. Desmond Ryan, *The Rising* (Dublin: Golden Eagle Books, 1949), p. 124. Cf. L. A. G. Strong's observation: "The last time I was with you, you told at the dinner table the magnificent death of the O'Rahilly. 'I helped to wind this clock, and must be there when it strikes,' you repeated, two or three times, and on to the noble conclusion 'Here died the O'Rahilly, R. I. P.'. . . ." *A Letter to W. B. Yeats* (London: Hogarth Press, 1932), p. 26.

36. Holt, *Protest in Arms*, p. 114.

37. Arnold Bax, *Farewell My Youth* (London: Longmans, Green, 1943), p. 100.

38. *The Golden Nightingale*, p. 60.

NOTES TO CHAPTER SEVEN

1. My analysis and interpretation of the sequence differs in significant respects from those of the two principal commentators: see Vivienne Koch, *W. B. Yeats: The Tragic Phase*, pp. 129-45; Edward B. Partridge, "Yeats's 'The Three Bushes'—Genesis and Structure," *Accent* 17 (1957): 67-80. My conclusions are not evident in Miss Koch's treatment; one of them is very barely suggested in Partridge's. In brief, they concern the existential isolation of the *personae* and the consequences that may be drawn therefrom. Also, I offer conclusions not embodied in the work of my predecessors on the relation of this sequence to Yeats's work and ideas as a whole. Partridge's aims are different from mine in that he is concerned primarily with the immediate biographical context of the poems and the musical structure ("contrapuntal") of the sequence; while my intention, aside from extensive textual explication, is to discover an emergent dominant idea, elicit from it related ideas, and relate them to a specific thesis concerning the development of Yeats's world view.

2. "Old Age of a Poet," *Kenyon Review* 2 (1940): 346.

3. See "Coda: The Verse of Yeats's Last Years," *Arizona Quarterly* 17 (1961): 63-68. George Brandon Saul argues that Yeats's last poems are so severely wanting in taste, tone, and import that our concern with them must be "largely a historical or biographical one, justified by the conviction of essential magnitude" induced by our reading of his earlier work. Among others, Saul's contention that by 1934 "the period of the great sequences had passed" is, I would insist, open to strong disagreement.

4. On his return from Spain late in the spring of 1936 Yeats spent a few days with Dorothy Wellesley, at which time they discussed their common theme. From 22 June 1936 to 28 November 1936 their correspondence includes frequent references to their projects—the two poems mentioned above and the subsequent lyrics composed by Yeats. Many of the letters contain drafts of the poems. For Dorothy

Wellesley's poem see the errata sheet in the December issue of *Broadsides* (Dublin: Cuala Press, 1937).

5. Though Yeats told Dorothy Wellesley (*DW*, p. 104), "When we meet we will decide upon the name of the fourteenth or fifteenth century fabulist who made the original story," no one has been able to trace either the "fabulist" or his book. For good reason, perhaps, not only because "Bourdeille" is a pun on *bordel* ("brothel"), as Miss Koch (*W. B. Yeats: The Tragic Phase*, p. 131) has indicated, but also because *bourde* means "fib," "humbug." On the other hand, Yeats may have known of Pierre de Bourdeille, abbé et seigneur de Brantôme (ca. 1540–1614), a *bon vivant* who, after suffering a severe fall from a horse (see details of Yeats's poem), chronicled often fancifully and usually extremely frankly the lives of numerous interesting personages.

6. "Ribh Denounces Patrick," originally entitled "Ribh Prefers an Older Theology." "Labouring heavens" recalls "Godhead on Godhead in sexual spasm begot/Godhead" of "Ribh in Ecstasy."

7. See the closing lines of *A Full Moon in March*.

8. This crucial word from "Sailing to Byzantium" I read not only as a synonym for "mortal" but also as a sexual metaphor in the sense of "longing intensely" and the older "experiencing orgasm." (Note that "generations" also has a sexual aspect.)

9. See "Among School Children" and Aristophanes' speech (189 ff.) in Plato's *Symposium*.

10. Henn, *The Lonely Tower*, pp. 313-14.

11. "We free ourselves from obsession that we may be nothing. The last kiss is given to the void." Letter of 17 April 1929 to Sturge Moore; Bridge, p. 154.

12. God here, of course, is not to be understood in the commonly received Judaeo–Christian sense. John Unterecker, who has shared with me his ideas on the theme of this paragraph, terms him "the divine whole hole."

13. *DW*, p. 118.

14. For Dorothy Wellesley's objection to the worm image and Yeats's defense of it, and for the original draft of the poem, see *DW*, pp. 116, 118.

15. From notes taken at the time. Quoted by A. Norman Jeffares in *W. B. Yeats, Man and Poet*, p. 267. Cf. *DW*, p. 192.

16. In *Civilization and its Discontents* Freud writes: "At the height of being in love the boundary between ego and object threatens to melt away. Against all the evidence of his senses, a man who is in love declares that 'I' and 'you' are one, and is prepared to behave as if it were a fact." *The Standard Edition of the Complete Psychological Works of Sigmund Freud*, trans. and ed. by James Strachey (London, 1961), XXI, 6.

17. Introduction to *The Resurrection*, in *Explorations*, p. 397.

18. *W. B. Yeats: The Tragic Phase*, p. 135.

✳ WORKS CITED

Auden, W. H. *Homage to Clio*. New York: Random House, 1960.

Bax, Arnold. *Farewell My Youth*. London: Longmans, Green, 1943.

Bradford, Curtis. *Yeats at Work*. Carbondale: Southern Illinois University Press, 1965.

———. "Yeats's Byzantium Poems: A Study of their Development," *PMLA* 75 (1960): 110-25.

Ellmann, Richard. *The Identity of Yeats*. London: Macmillan, 1954.

Freud, Sigmund. *Civilization and its Discontents*. Vol. XXI of *The Standard Edition of the Complete Psychological Works of Sigmund Freud*. Translated and edited by James Strachey. London: Hogarth Press and the Institute of Psychoanalysis, 1961.

Gogarty, Oliver St. John. *William Butler Yeats: A Memoir*. Dublin: Dolmen Press, 1963.

Gregory, Isabella Augusta. *Lady Gregory's Journals, 1916–1930*. Edited by Lennox Robinson. London: Putnam, 1946.

Gwynn, Stephen (ed.). *Scattering Branches*. New York: Macmillan, 1940.

Hall, James, and Steinmann, Martin (eds.). *The Permanence of Yeats*. New York: Macmillan, 1950.

Henn, T. R. "The Accent of Yeats' 'Last Poems,'" *Essays and Studies*. Vol. IX (N.S.), 1956. Collected for the English Association by Sir George Rostrevor Hamilton. London: John Murray, 1956. Pp. 56-72.

———. *The Lonely Tower*. London: Methuen, 1950.

Holt, Edgar. *Protest in Arms*. London: Putnam, 1960.

Hone, Joseph. *W. B. Yeats, 1865–1939*. London: Macmillan, 1942.

———. "Yeats as Political Philosopher," *London Mercury* 39 (1939): 492-96.

Jeffares, A. Norman. "The Byzantine Poems of Yeats," *Review of English Studies* 22 (1946): 44-52.

———. "Notes on Yeats's 'Lapis Lazuli,'" *Modern Language Notes* 65 (1950): 488-91.

———. *W. B. Yeats, Man and Poet*. New Haven: Yale University Press, 1949.

———. "Yeats' 'The Gyres': Sources and Symbolism," *Huntington Library Quarterly* 15 (1951): 89-97.

Joyce, James. *A Portrait of the Artist as a Young Man*. New York: Modern Library, n.d.

———. *Stephen Hero*. Edited by Theodore Spencer. Norfolk, Conn.: New Directions, 1944.

Kermode, Frank. *Romantic Image*. New York: Macmillan, 1957.

Koch, Vivienne. *W. B. Yeats: The Tragic Phase*. London: Routledge and Kegan Paul, 1951.

Macardle, Dorothy. *The Irish Republic*. Dublin: Irish Press, 1951.

MacBride, Maud Gonne. *A Servant of the Queen*. London: Gollancz, 1938.

Maloney, William J. *The Forged Casement Diaries*. Dublin: Talbot Press, 1936.

Miller, Liam, ed. *The Dolmen Press Yeats Centenary Papers*. Dublin: Dolmen Press, 1968.

Moore, Virginia. *The Unicorn*. New York: Macmillan, 1954.

Noyes, Alfred. *The Accusing Ghost of Roger Casement*. London: Gollancz, 1957.

———. *Two Worlds for Memory*. London: Sheed and Ward, 1953.

O'Connor, Frank. *The Fountain of Magic*. London: Macmillan, 1939.

———. *Kings, Lords & Commons*. New York: Knopf, 1959.

———. *Lords and Commons*. Dublin: Cuala Press, 1938.

———. *An Only Child*. New York: Knopf, 1961.

———. "The Old Age of a Poet," *The Bell* 1 (1941): 7-18.

———. "Two Friends: Yeats and AE," *Yale Review* 29 (1939): 60-88.

———. *The Wild Bird's Nest*. Dublin: Cuala Press, 1932.

Parkinson, Thomas. *W. B. Yeats, Self-Critic*. Berkeley: University of California Press, 1951.

Parrish, Stephen Maxfield (ed.). *A Concordance to the Poems of W. B. Yeats*. Ithaca: Cornell University Press, 1963.

Partridge, Edward B. "Yeats's 'The Three Bushes'—Genesis and Structure," *Accent* 17 (1957): 67-80.

Pound, Ezra. *Gaudier-Brzeska, A Memoir*. London: John Lane, 1916.

R., D. *Irish Independent*, 4 May 1957.

Raglan, Fitzroy Richard Somerset, 4th Baron. *The Hero*. New York: Vintage Books, 1956.

Ransom, John Crowe. "Old Age of a Poet," *Kenyon Review* 2 (1940): 345-47.

Robinson, Lennox (ed.). *The Irish Theatre*. London: Macmillan, 1939.

Ryan, Desmond. *The Rising*. Dublin: Golden Eagle Books, 1949.

Saul, George Brandon. "Coda: The Verse of Yeats's Last Years," *Arizona Quarterly* 17 (1961): 63-68.

———. *Prolegomena to the Study of Yeats's Poems*. Philadelphia: University of Pennsylvania Press, 1957.

Scott-James, R. A. "Editorial Notes," *London Mercury* 39 (1939): 477-80.

Singleton-Gates, Peter, and Girodias, Maurice. *The Black Diaries of Roger Casement*. New York: Grove Press, 1959.

Stallworthy, Jon. *Between the Lines: W. B. Yeats's Poetry in the Making*. Oxford: Clarendon Press, 1963.

———. *Vision and Revision in Yeats's "Last Poems."* London: Oxford University Press, 1969.

Stauffer, Donald. *The Golden Nightingale*. New York: Macmillan, 1949.

Strong, L. A. G. *A Letter to W. B. Yeats*. London: Hogarth Press, 1932.

Tindall, William York. *Forces in Modern British Literature, 1885–1956*. New York: Vintage Books, 1956.

———. *The Literary Symbol*. New York: Columbia University Press, 1955.

———. Review of *Kings, Lords & Commons*, by Frank O'Connor, *New York Herald Tribune Book Review*, 2 August 1959, p. 5.

Unterecker, John. *A Reader's Guide to William Butler Yeats*. New York: Noonday Press, 1959.

———. (ed.). *Yeats: A Collection of Critical Essays*. Englewood Cliffs, N.J.: Prentice-Hall, 1963.

Virgil. *The Pastoral Poems*. Translated by E. V. Rieu. London: Penguin, 1949.

Winters, Yvor. "The Poetry of W. B. Yeats," *Twentieth Century Literature* 6 (1960): 3-24.

Yeats, John Butler. *Letters to His Son W. B. Yeats and Others, 1869–1922*. Edited by Joseph Hone. London: Faber and Faber, 1944.

Yeats, Michael. "W. B. Yeats and Irish Folk Song," *Southern Folklore Quarterly* 31 (1966): 153-78.

Yeats, William Butler. *Autobiographies*. London: Macmillan, 1955.

———. *Explorations*. London: Macmillan, 1962.

———. *Essays and Introductions*. London: Macmillan, 1961.

———. *John Sherman and Dhoya*. London: Unwin, 1891. (Published under the pseudonym "Ganconagh.")

———. *The Letters of W. B. Yeats*. Edited by Allan Wade. New York: Macmillan, 1955.

———. *Letters on Poetry from W. B. Yeats to Dorothy Wellesley*. London: Oxford University Press, 1940.

———. *Mythologies*. London: Macmillan, 1959.

————. *Plays and Controversies.* London: Macmillan, 1923.

————. *The Variorum Edition of the Poems of W. B. Yeats.* Edited by Peter Allt and Russell K. Alspach. New York: Macmillan, 1957.

————. *A Vision.* New York: Macmillan, 1938.

————. *W. B. Yeats and T. Sturge Moore: Their Correspondence, 1901–1937.* Edited by Ursula Bridge. New York: Oxford University Press, 1953.

Yeats, William Butler (ed.). *A Book of Irish Verse.* London: Methuen, 1900.

———— (ed.). *The Oxford Book of Modern Verse.* Oxford: Clarendon Press, 1936.

————, and Higgins, F. R. (eds.). *Broadsides.* Dublin: Cuala Press, 1935.

————, and Wellesley, Dorothy (eds.). *Broadsides.* Dublin: Cuala Press, 1937.

✳ INDEX

A Note on the Type

Beyond Byzantium was designed by John B. Goetz. The text was set in Linotype *Janson* with display lines in *Janson* and *Deepdene*. The paper is Beckett White Laid Text, the cloth, Bancroft Buckram. The book was printed and bound by the Pantagraph Press, Bloomington, Illinois.